MASTERS OF INEQUALITY

50 years after our cities burned, why American society is still so divided, and what we must do <u>now</u> to avoid chronic conflict.

By Andre F. Shashaty

Masters of Inequality

Partnership for Sustainable Communities
914 Mission Ave., Suite 4A
San Rafael, CA 94901

Ordering Information:
Quantity sales. Special discounts are available on quantity purchases by corporations, associations, and others.
Orders by U.S. trade bookstores and wholesalers. Call 415-453-2100 x 303.

Printed in the United States of America

Publisher's Cataloging-In-Publication Data
Shashaty, Andre.

Masters of Inequality: 50 years after our cities burned, why American society is still so divided, and what we must do now to avoid chronic conflict.

ISBN 978-0-9905187-2-3

1. urban policy—housing – United States
2. U.S. Department of Housing and Urban Development.
3. race relations – racial segregation
4. affordable housing
5. sustainability – sustainable communities
6. economic inequality

First Edition
14 13 12 11 10 / 10 9 8 7 6 5 4 3 2 1

On the Cover

U.S. Army troops, one with a machine gun, stand guard on the steps of the U.S. Senate wing of the Capitol Building in Washington, D.C., on April 5, 1968. They were part of a deployment of 11,570 troops called into the nation's capital by order of President Lyndon Johnson during a period of arson and looting following the assassination of Dr. Martin Luther King, Jr. in Memphis, Tenn., April 4. The flag is at half staff in tribute to the civil rights leader. (AP Photo)

Dedication

This book is dedicated to a group of government employees who generally get no recognition at all: The people who now serve or have served at the U.S. Department of Housing and Urban Development. Since 1979, I've met more than 100 staffers from that agency, and I know that they and their colleagues have done good work under difficult circumstances. I am particularly proud to have known the men and women who gave up good jobs in the private sector to take positions at HUD, accepting the heavy weight of government red tape and making the sacrifice of taking lower pay (in many cases). Some of them even relocated to Washington, D.C., from homes elsewhere to provide important leadership. They are the unsung heroes of the struggle to provide housing and improve communities that has been going on for 50 years as this book went to press. I hope their work is continued, and receives the respect it deserves from the U.S. Congress and from future occupants of the White House.

Andre F. Shashaty

Acknowledgements

I am grateful for all the help I received to write and publish this book. My sincere appreciation goes to the following people:

My wife Lesley for encouragement and proofreading.

Robert Bradford, John Lowry, Alicia Mosley, and Wesley Palmer for help with preparation of the manuscript.

Kay Marshall for typesetting and graphic design, and Dennis Whitehead for photo research.

Dr. Laverne Joseph and Retirement Housing Foundation for supporting our nonprofit's educational efforts on housing issues.

Betty Pagett and Patrick Sheridan for consistent help organizing and running the Partnership for Sustainable Communities.

Paul A. Jargowsky, Douglas Massey, Clay Risen, Wendell E. Pritchett, Patrick Sharkey, Kenneth Stahl, Robert Weaver and other researchers and authors who documented housing and urban issues in America.

Andre F. Shashaty

Table of Contents

Preface

President Barack Obama and hundreds of other dignitaries marked the 50th anniversary of the 1965 Selma-to-Montgomery voting rights march by reenacting the most dramatic part of the event. They commemorated a crucial step in the progress toward civil rights in the South.

It would be tempting to forget that it has also been a half-century since a far more disturbing series of events unfolded in the North in the 1960s, events connected to a different phase of the civil rights struggle.

From the summer of 1965 through the spring of 1968, a series of violent upheavals left at least 130 people dead, over 4,000 injured, thousands of buildings destroyed, and hundreds of millions of dollars in wages and tax revenue lost.

The devastation was not the result of foreign invaders or terrorist attacks. Americans were fighting other Americans on the streets of cities across the country. Noncombatants ran for their lives or hid in their cellars. Fires destroyed entire city blocks. Soldiers patrolled with mounted bayonets. Choking smoke and tear gas filled the air. Snipers fired from rooftops, and soldiers responded with torrents of deadly gunfire.

In city after city, local and state police were quickly overwhelmed, and National Guard troops were deployed. In several cities, convoys of regular U.S. Army troops took up positions. Soldiers mounted machine guns on the steps of the U.S. Capitol. Army troops from the 3rd Infantry guarded the White House.

The underlying cause of the 1960s riots, like most rebellions in human history, was the widening gap between the haves and the have-nots. In the 1960s, people of color had many grievances about how they were treated by white institutions, including their local police departments.

But when sociologists and government officials drilled down to the core of what made so many people so angry, they found one thing that affected everyone in communities of color, especially children: residential segregation and terrible living conditions.

Millions of African Americans, many who had migrated from the South to seek better lives in northern cities, were herded into what used to be called ghettos – overcrowded, poor, and decaying places that encapsulated and perpetuated all the injustices they had suffered.

These were places with terrible schools, large numbers of teenagers who had dropped out, and high unemployment. Many people lived in substandard housing run by slumlords, endured high crime, and paid way too much of their income for rent.

Worst of all, for many African Americans, the ghettos were traps from which escape was hard if not impossible. Even the most financially successful people faced a long struggle to find housing outside these hellholes.

For those who have not faced discrimination or been denied the chance to live where we choose, including myself, it's hard to fully grasp what it was like. But it's important to try.

Historians describe Levittown, the huge housing development on New York's Long Island, as the prototype for the idyllic suburban "bedroom community." Completed in 1951, it epitomized the "good life" of the postwar era, a place where Mr. and Mrs. America could afford a house with a yard, a picket fence, and two cars in the driveway.

But for black families, that vision was a dream that almost never came true, and few dared even dream it. They were not allowed to buy at Levittown or at many other developments like it in other cities. It did not matter if they had the money to do so or not. The newest developments were overwhelmingly all-white communities; no blacks were allowed.

Integration interrupted

Rulings requiring desegregation of public facilities and establishing the right to vote in the South were widely accepted. Nonetheless, white Americans stoutly resisted the idea that blacks and whites should live in close proximity, especially in the North.

Real estate agents and banks collaborated to keep black families from buying existing homes in white areas. If they could not be kept out of an area, real estate agents fanned the fears of white property owners about integration. This would lead to a wave of panic selling and so-called white flight. The cities became blacker, and the suburbs became whiter.

Big city governments lost tax revenue and began to cut already inadequate services to the ghettos. Inner city schools were badly overcrowded. Sanitation services were inadequate, and building code violations were rarely corrected. Crime and unemployment were rampant.

Government programs and policies made segregation worse. Federal grants were used to clear land for major commercial developments, often destroying low-cost housing and displacing its residents. Inner city residents rarely had the political power to fight the loss of their homes, and were rarely given relocation assistance.

In many cities, blacks had grown as a percentage of the population but had little or no voice in decisions that affected them, and were often thwarted in the pursuit of elected office.

There were ample warnings that the frustration, anger and hopelessness would explode, and in August of 1965, it did.

Watts explodes

A dispute between black residents and white police over a traffic stop escalated, and the Watts area of Los Angeles erupted in flames, looting and shooting. Some people called for rebellion against what they charged was a racist city government. The fires and the violence raged for six days, resulting in 34 deaths and the destruction, damage, or looting of 1,000 buildings.

In 1966, race riots in Chicago and Cleveland required National Guard troops to restore order. Other cities felt the heat that year, too.

In June 1967, Tampa, Fla., erupted in violence. Before it was over, a riot had started in Cincinnati, Ohio. That was followed by trouble in Atlanta, and then in Newark, a riot that *Life* magazine called "a shooting war in the streets." In a city now known mostly as a major airline hub, the New Jersey National Guard and state police fired 13,326 rounds of ammunition in three days of violence.

The highest death toll came in Detroit, where looting and burning of buildings gave way to snipers firing at police and firemen as rioting spread from the west side to the east side.

There were 41 substantial disturbances in 39 cities, resulting in 83 deaths, according to a Senate committee that investigated urban problems.

The first few months of 1968 brought the hope that the worst was behind us. Then came April. The murder of Martin Luther King, Jr., on April 4 threw black districts of cities all over America into bitter, anguished mourning.

In the black ghettos of New York City, Indianapolis and many other cities, grief was expressed peacefully. However, there was violence in communities from coast to coast. In 20 cities, the violence was bad enough to require the presence of National Guard troops and/or regular U.S. Army soldiers.

In Washington, D.C., federal office workers fled for fear of their lives, jamming the bridges to Virginia so badly that many abandoned their cars and walked. Rioters came within blocks of the White House.

Entire sections of these cities looked like war zones, with burned-out buildings surrounded by piles of rubble. Unknown thousands of people fled their homes or businesses, some never to return. The flight of white households from the central cities to the suburbs accelerated.

Some of the affected neighborhoods did not return to economic vitality for 30 or 40 years after the riots. The political and social damage would last even longer, as fear and mistrust between the races became entrenched.

• • •

The Detroit fires were still smoldering when President Johnson appointed a blue ribbon commission to study the causes of the riots. The National Advisory Commission on Civil Disorders (known as the Kerner Commission for its chairman, Otto Kerner, Jr.) issued its findings on February 29, 1968.

The report said the riots were a predictable reaction to the terrible conditions in the inner cities, and that those conditions were created by white institutions and condoned by white citizens. In very blunt language, it blamed "white racism" for creating the conditions that invited violence.

The report called for, among other things, massive federal spending to provide integrated affordable housing so that central cities would not become mostly black while outlying neighborhoods and suburbs remained overwhelmingly white.

King called the Kerner Commission report "a diagnosis of death with a prescription for life."

I have written this book because that prescription has not been filled.

The conditions that engendered the anger that fueled the 1960s riots are still with us, and the political divisions over what the government should do about it are just as extreme now as they were 50 years ago.

It's not that we haven't made progress. We have. Blatant discrimination in the rental or sale of housing is illegal now. We created the U.S. Department of Housing and Urban Development, known as HUD, and equipped it with programs funded with tens of billions of dollars each year.

However, the progress has not been sufficient. For every step forward, there has been a half step backwards – or worse. The most devastating reversal came when the surge in predatory home mortgage lending in the early 2000s precipitated the foreclosure crisis, which was followed by the Great Recession.

This double-disaster hit people of color the hardest. Mortgage lenders had targeted minority neighborhoods for predatory loans, and foreclosures hit those areas like a tsunami of economic devastation.

Then came the current era of budget austerity in Congress and in state capitals. Several very important housing programs were eliminated. Deep cuts were made in existing benefits that helped people pay rent for privately owned housing.

For years, the federal government and many states have been in full-blown retreat from the commitment to cities made by Johnson and the Congress in the 1960s.

The net effect has been to reverse much of the progress made in the '70s, '80s and '90s in our cities. The shortage of affordable housing has hit crisis proportions, and the number of homeless has set new records.

Inner city areas and now some inner-ring suburbs are decaying and suffering from the disinvestment that followed the increase in foreclosures.

Segregation has been stubbornly persistent in America. The prevalence of areas of concentrated poverty has increased, with all the dysfunction it brings. Millions of children grow up in these places, places that used to be called ghettos. Sociologists now call them "high-poverty neighborhoods." They are America's factories of inequality.

• • •

I have written this book knowing it would not be popular. It deals with what appears to be an intractable problem, one that arouses strong feelings and is not easy to talk about.

I have done it because I believe there is hope for progress. The millennial generation, those young adults born in the 1980s to the early 2000s, is a powerful force for change. This group is showing much more concern about social justice and racial equality than their parents did.

They have not bought into their parents' belief that a house is primarily an investment rather than shelter, and that it has to be protected by walls, whether physical or legal, to keep out people of lower incomes or people of color.

They have been outraged by recent killings of unarmed black men by white police. They have protested racial injustice in the towns and campuses where they live. They have carried signs and chanted loudly to say, "black lives matter."

What they need to know is that for a brief time back in the '60s, a powerful alliance of political leaders not only agreed with that principle, they acted on it. They recognized that far-reaching action was needed to address police brutality (as it was called then), but also a much wider range of social, political, and economic issues, including the fundamental problem of housing discrimination.

The Kerner Commission warned that, if we did not act decisively, the division of Americans into two societies, one black and one white, could soon become permanent. It said that fear, mistrust, and violence would become pervasive, and costs for social welfare, prisons and law enforcement would keep going up.

Divisions continue

Today, the racial divide continues to exist and grow, and while it may be less obvious, it's still powerful. Although there is less blatant discrimination solely on the basis of race, there is more by class and income. The dire shortage of affordable housing hurts all people who have meager resources, and it's getting worse every day.

The visionaries of the '60s recognized that decent housing and healthy neighborhoods affordable and open to people of all incomes and races are the most effective foundation for reducing inequality and helping people advance their own fortunes.

The challenge for the millennials – and those of us who share their idealism – is to get that message across in Washington, D.C., and our state capitals, and finally, in our own backyards, where the debate over housing and opportunity is affected by decisions made every day.

Over the coming months, as the 50th anniversary of each of the riots arrives, we must not take the easy route and pretend that they did not happen. Acknowledging what occurred and how we reacted is vitally important to understanding the racial and social issues we face today and for deciding where we go from here.

The process of electing a new president and Congress makes such discussion even more crucial. Powerful political forces are mobilizing to terminate spending on housing and urban programs and to roll back federal and state efforts to enforce fair housing laws. If they are empowered in the coming election, there may be no way to avoid continued conflict and division.

In the 1960s, for a brief time, we were inspired to seek a better society – a single society that was not divided along racial and economic lines – with opportunity for all. That vision of America has been under attack in many ways for many years. As you read this book and begin to see how we got to this point, I hope it will help you draw your own conclusions about where we are headed, and what we can do about it.

For more information on the organization of this book and its author, see "About this book" and "About the author" in the back of the book. The page numbers are listed on the Table of Contents.

SECTION ONE

Exodus & Upheaval

CHAPTER ONE

The Struggle Moves North

In June 1951, the owner of an apartment building in Cicero, Ill., defied the strict housing segregation in the Chicago area and rented an apartment to a black bus driver and World War II veteran named Harvey E. Clark, Jr. When Clark, his wife and his two children tried to move in, police told them they could not live there because of their race. If Clark returned, the police chief warned, he'd be shot.

But Clark did return, this time with a federal court order prohibiting police interference. On July 11, 1951, despite the anger and threats of the local citizens, he moved in. As night fell, a crowd of 4,000 or so gathered with the intention of forcing Clark to flee. They attacked the building with bricks, bottles and rocks, ransacked part of it, and tried to set it on fire.

When the Cicero police failed to disperse the crowd, Gov. Adlai Stevenson mobilized the Illinois National Guard. The troops used bayonets and the butts of their rifles to clear the area around the building and erected a barbed wire perimeter.

The violence in Cicero was particularly vicious, but it was only one of many times black families who dared to move into white areas of Chicago were threatened, harassed or attacked. And Chicago was only one of the major cities where housing segregation was enforced at the points of guns and knives, or more often, with fusillades of rocks or eggs.

A number of dramas and documentaries have commemorated the success of nonviolent civil rights activists in the South. But what few Americans recognize is that the civil rights struggle did not end when blacks won voting rights in the South. It simply moved north, where it focused on housing and communities instead of voting and access to public facilities. And when it arrived, it was met with a level of hatred and violence that shocked even Martin Luther King, Jr.

Northerners liked to think of themselves as more tolerant than southerners. Some held true to that self image, but as the black population of northern cities grew, many did not.

The mainstream media does not like to look back at the details of the conflict between blacks and whites in the North. However, the racial conflict and division that erupted back then still reverberate throughout our nation. The housing segregation today is less rigid and absolute, but it is still an entrenched fact of life in many parts of the North. The inner city areas that used to be called ghettos still suffer from severe problems, and political choices being made now are making them worse.

To start to understand the depth and intensity of the conflict, it's important to look back at the gulf between northern whites who feared and resented change, and the millions of African Americans who had come North looking for a better life.

Northern whites had little experience dealing with blacks before World War II ended. Neither they nor their elected officials were prepared for what became known as the "great migration" – the relocation of millions of blacks from the South to the North in two great waves, one after World War I and another that started after World War II and continued well into the '60s.

More than 6 million African Americans moved from the rural South to the cities of the North, Midwest and West from 1916 to 1970. In 1900, 90 percent of black Americans lived in the South, most of them on farms. By 1970, less than half of American blacks remained living in the South. The vast majority of those who moved North lived in central cities.

They came in search of jobs in the booming industries of the northern cities where they expected to make much more than what they could make in agriculture down South. They dreamed of greater racial tolerance, and of escaping subservience and random violence.

The new southern arrivals were mostly from rural areas and were generally poor and poorly educated. Many of them were from the Deep South, spoke with a distinctly southern dialect and had different social and cultural standards and practices[1].

The human wave presented a huge challenge for northern cities, their citizens and their governments. Even the black families that were already established in the north did not know what to make of the influx of southern blacks, according to Robert Weaver, a black sociologist, author, and U.S. government official.

It created a demand for housing that had a profound effect on northern cities because there was very little provision by local, state or federal government to help house them. Throughout the 1950s, construction of housing in central cities had not come close to keeping up with demand.

At first, the newcomers gathered in existing black districts. But

---

"An Exodus from the South"

Articles in the African American newspapers of the 1920s provide insight into what "the Great Migration" was like. As reported in the Savannah (Ga.) Tribune, the promise of a better life in the North was a powerful attraction to millions of southerners. The South was a terrible place for blacks in the years prior to the civil rights advancements in the '60s. It was also a tough place to make a living. The newspaper described the excitement as rural folks from all over the South converged on train stations to make the trip up North. There'd be jobs, and they'd be treated like regular citizens, at least relative to how they had been treated in the South.

In an article on Dec. 28, 1922, on the state of African-Americans, the paper said that even in the winter months, a survey of "the great railway centers" showed that there was "an exodus from the South." The paper also carried the news of the dedication in Washington, D.C., of the memorial to Abraham Lincoln, the Great Emancipator who gave African Americans the freedom of movement to head north, or wherever they chose to go.

---

as those areas became overcrowded, the stage was set for intensifying conflict between blacks struggling to find more space and better living conditions and whites who were intent on keeping them from moving out of the ghettos.

Over time, with overcrowding, economic exploitation by property owners, and poor city services, the black neighborhoods deteriorated. Financially successful black families saved money in hopes of escaping the overcrowded slums. But time after time, they were told in the most hostile ways that they were not welcome anywhere else.

In the South, whites and blacks often interacted. But for whites in the northern cities, black people were an unknown quantity. They responded to them with fear, distrust, and in many cases, hostility.

To many northerners, it was fine to say blacks should be allowed to vote, but it was quite another thing to say they should be allowed to live in the same neighborhoods as whites. Most northern communities were rigidly segregated, and the more black citizens arrived, the more whites defended their separation. In most newly developed communities, homes were not for sale to blacks.

If a black family inquired about a home for sale, the price of the house would suddenly jump 100 percent, or the house would be taken off the market.

One of the most common methods used to keep a neighborhood from becoming integrated was the restrictive covenant. This was a provision inserted in the deed for a property that prohibited the buyer or any future owner from ever selling the property to black people.

When a broker or rental agent found out that someone inquiring about a home was black, he or she suddenly became evasive and full of excuses about why a property listed in the paper was not suitable for the person inquiring.

If a white homeowner agreed to sell a property to a black family, he or she often backed out after facing angry reactions or vandalism from neighbors.

If a black family did succeed in buying a house or obtaining a lease for an apartment in a white neighborhood, they were treated with contempt and threatened.

Even Jackie Robinson, the first black player in major league baseball, was rebuffed repeatedly when he tried to buy a home in the Connecticut suburbs of New York City. He and his wife were repeatedly told that homes that had been advertised had suddenly become unavailable when they inquired. They only succeeded in buying in Connecticut when prominent white citizens decided that discriminating against a world famous sports hero was generating too much bad publicity.

The Robinson family's experience is reflected in the sociological research of the time.

In the 1950s, sociologists developed a measurement for how severely a city is segregated. It is called the dissimilarity index. It captures in a standardized measurement the degree to which two racial groups are integrated or segregated by neighborhood (or more technically, census tract).

The index ranges from 0 to 100. The numbers represent the estimated percentage of one group that would have to move so that every tract in the city would have the same proportions of each group as the city as a whole. A value of 60 or above is considered very high segregation. Values of 40 to 50 are considered moderate levels of segregation, while values of 30 or less are considered low.

In 1960, in the nation's largest 207 cities, the average segregation index was 86.2.[2] That means that 86 percent of blacks would have needed to move in order to achieve the proportions of white and black households in every neighborhood that were the same as the proportions for the cities overall.

King comes to Chicago

Housing segregation was the norm in many northern cities, but it was particularly entrenched in Chicago. That's why it was the perfect city for the application of nonviolent protest to attract national attention to the issue.

In January 1966, Martin Luther King, Jr., moved into a dilapidated apartment on the West Side of the city to emphasize his commitment to help local leaders end segregation and improve the conditions in the slums. In July of that year, 35,000 people gathered at Chicago's Soldier Field to begin the Chicago Freedom Movement, also known as the "open housing movement."

King led a march to Chicago City Hall, where he and his allies posted a list of demands for open housing and improvements in the slums. The demands included some very obvious things, like improved garbage collection, regular street cleaning, and enforcement of building codes – all things that white neighborhoods took for granted.

The movement also called for mortgage lenders to provide loans to any qualified borrower without regard to the racial composition of the area where a home was located. Real estate brokers were asked to make all homes available on a nondiscriminatory basis.

King and his local allies asked the Chicago Housing Authority to stop concentrating poor blacks in high-rise public housing complexes and instead provide public housing in low-rise buildings dispersed throughout a variety of neighborhoods

It had been 15 years since the Cicero riot, but King knew hostility toward "open housing" was still intense. Undeterred, he and local advocates marched right into the heart of neighborhoods where opposition to integrated housing was strongest.

King was a veteran of violent reactions to civil rights protests in the South, but he was surprised by the degree of hostility and violence he would face in the Windy City.

One of the marches against housing discrimination took place in the white community of South Dearing on August 21, 1966. Between 1,000 and 2,000 white residents lined the streets. They threw bricks, stones, and bottles at protesters. Someone threw a stone that hit King in the head. A knife was thrown, narrowly missing the civil rights leader. King said the people in Chicago were more hateful than any he'd encountered down South.

After a series of protests, an agreement was reached with the city of Chicago and the Chicago Real Estate Board that met some of the movement's demands. But many fundamental problems would continue for decades after King's death.

Chicagoans made their feelings about integration painfully clear, in person and in the newspaper headlines of the day. In most other American cities, much the same thing was going on, but with less violence and publicity.

In California, in what was to become Silicon Valley, segregated housing was the norm. Black families had little or no chance of buying a home in Palo Alto, the location of Stanford University and birthplace of the tech industry. If they held jobs in the area south of San Francisco, they had one choice: the community of East Palo Alto.

One of the men who remembered those days, an Air Force veteran named Bob Hoover, recalled how housing segregation worked. He'd call and ask if an apartment advertised for rent in Palo Alto was still available. The person on the phone would say "yes." But when he showed up, and the landlord saw he was black, they would say it had been rented.[3]

That's the mundane but very widespread reality of how housing segregation was perpetuated then, and to a lesser extent, still is today.

• • •

King wrote about the struggle for open housing in his book, *Where Do We Go From Here: Chaos or Community?* Published in 1968, the year he died, it was his attempt to lay out ideas for how blacks and whites could learn to live together.

"Nothing today more clearly indicates the residue of racism still lodging in our society than the responses of white America to integrated housing. Here the tides of prejudice, fear and irrationality rise to flood proportions," King wrote.

King explained that problems of education, transportation, jobs, and decent living conditions were all made more difficult "because housing was so rigidly segregated."

The civil rights leader deconstructed the "blame the victim" logic that whites used to explain why they supported housing segregation even though they did not think of themselves as racists:

> Many whites who oppose open housing would deny that they are racists. They turn to sociological arguments – the crime rate in the Negro community, the lagging cultural standards, the fear that their schools will become academically inferior, the fear that property values will depreciate – in order to find excuses for their opposition. They never stop to realize that criminal responses are environmental, not racial. To hem a people up in the prison walls of overcrowded ghettos and to confine them in rat-infested slums is to breed crime, whatever the racial group may be. It is a strange and twisted logic to use the tragic results of segregation as an argument for its continuation.
>
> *–Where Do We Go From Here: Chaos or Community?*

Children and education

Housing segregation and school segregation are closely related.

Some Americans may be tempted to think that our schools were desegregated in the 1960s. After all, history classes taught us that blacks won the right to attend school with white children after the Supreme Court ruling in Brown v. Board of Education.

But what history books generally don't teach is that the court ruling directly affected only certain kinds of segregation in schools. Down South, black and white children often lived in close proximity to each other. Schools were usually segregated by law or custom, not because the two groups lived miles apart in separate school districts. Thus, when the courts outlawed school segregation, and those policies were changed, there was a fairly direct transition to mixed-race classrooms.

In the North, it was different. The strict segregation of housing dictated that black and white kids lived apart and attended different schools. Kids from black areas attended schools that were almost all black. White kids attended schools that were mostly white, or left public schools altogether. There was no legislative or legal "quick fix" to this pattern.

In the '60s and '70s, the only solution that advocates of integration could come up with was to haul kids across town on buses to attend schools where there was a mix of races in attendance. What became known as "forced busing" was wildly unpopular because of the disruption it caused. Charter and magnet schools have had some impact in recent years, but millions of black children attended heavily segregated and often overcrowded schools.

What was it like for those kids? An official government commission's report on conditions in Los Angeles described the dismal situation for ghetto children in the 1960s:[4]

> ...what has depressed and stunned us most is the dull, devastating spiral of failure that awaits the average disadvantaged child in the urban core. His home life all too often fails to give him the incentive and the elementary experience with words and ideas which prepares most children for school. Unprepared and unready, he may not learn to read or write at all...
>
> Two-thirds of those who enter the high schools (in the area studied) do not graduate, many of them slipping into the ranks of the permanent jobless, illiterate and untrained, unemployed and unemployable...
>
> Because of the low standard of achievement in the schools in the urban core and adjacent areas, parents of the better students from advantageous backgrounds remove them from these schools, either by changing the location of the family home or by sending the children to private school. In turn, the average achievement level of the schools in the disadvantaged area sinks lower and lower.

The public schools in many other cities were as bad or worse than those in L.A. In Detroit for example, 50 percent of the students in the city's high schools dropped out before graduating in the mid-'60s.

CHAPTER TWO

The Profits of Fear

Racial fear and bias drove the segregated housing patterns of mid-20th-century America. But greed also played a very important role. Players in the real estate industry often claimed that they simply responded to the wishes of their clients, the white property owners. However, the truth is that many of them actively orchestrated the complex system of housing segregation in order to make more money.

Discrimination prevented access to many non-slum areas, particularly the suburbs, where good housing existed and was not too expensive. It also created enormous demand for housing in the racial ghettos, making it possible for property owners to jack up rents of deteriorated ghetto housing higher than they would be in a truly free market.[5] Owners of apartment buildings could subdivide individual units to cram more people into each building, increasing their income even more.

For black families that aspired to homeownership, buying a house was like walking through a minefield of greedy and exploitative real estate industry tactics. Real estate brokers and speculators made huge profits exploiting the ambitions of blacks and the fears of whites. They understood that blacks who urgently wanted decent homes and whites hysterical about the influx of blacks were all ripe for the fleecing.

Ghetto slumlords often skimped on maintenance of their rental properties. Sometimes, they did not bother to provide heat or hot water. They often ignored calls from tenants to make repairs to plumbing and to plug holes where rats came in to the apartments. City building inspectors often failed to enforce building codes and order correction of code violations in these properties.

Since blacks were generally unable to move from the ghettos, they were at the mercy of these slumlords. They often paid more in rent than people in white neighborhoods for similar apartments – and endured worse conditions and less service.

King spoke about these conditions in one of his very last appearances before he died.

"I was in Newark and Harlem just this week," he said at Washington Cathedral on March 31, 1968. "I walked into the homes of welfare mothers, and I saw them in conditions – no not with wall-to-wall carpet – but wall-to-wall rats and roaches."

He explained how ghetto residents like the women in those cities often found it impossible to get their landlords to make repairs: "She showed me the holes where the rats came in. She said that, night after night, she had to stay awake to keep the rats and the roaches from getting to the children."

Housing conditions

In 1968, 56 percent of the country's nonwhite families lived in central cities and of those, nearly two-thirds lived in neighborhoods marked by substandard housing and general urban blight.[6] "For these citizens, condemned by segregation and poverty to live in the decaying slums of our central cities, the goal of a decent home and suitable living environment is as far distant as ever," a government inquiry stated.

For the U.S. as a whole, the trend was toward reduction in the percentage of housing units that were substandard, thanks to new construction in the suburbs. Most of that housing was for whites only. Within many central cities, the aging stock of low-cost housing continued to deteriorate.

Federal grants for redevelopment of urban areas made matters worse, since they usually resulted in the destruction of large numbers of low-cost homes to make way for commercial projects. This reduction in supply led directly to rent increases and overcrowding of the remaining apartments.

Many ghetto residents simply could not pay the rent necessary to obtain decent housing. In Detroit, for example, over 40 percent of the units occupied by nonwhites in 1960 required rent of over 35 percent of the tenants' income.

Landlords took full advantage of the lack of housing options for black families. In Newark, nonwhites with housing essentially the same as whites paid rents that were 8 percent to 17 percent higher than whites. This cost differential was known as the "color tax" and was part of daily life in most racial ghettos.[7]

The ownership trap

Black families that put together the money for a downpayment found that the American dream was often a nightmare. They were often charged more than a white family would be charged, both for the home itself and for the interest on the loan to buy it.

Most wanted to escape the ghetto, but it was rarely possible for them to find areas that offered a mix of people of various races for any length of time. Integration was slow to come to most neighborhoods, and when it did, it rarely lasted. White people rarely stuck around an area once blacks started to move in.

In many cases, this was not a spontaneous reaction but the result of a practice called "blockbusting." In the '50s and '60s, blockbusting was all about making money by spreading fear of black people among white homeowners. It was as easy as spreading the word that black people were moving into a neighborhood. It did not matter whether any had done so or not. The mere threat was enough to cause white people to retain brokers to sell their homes as quickly as possible.

The work could be done without a direct appeal to racism. A broker could say that he was just looking out for the homeowner's economic interests, since other owners would undoubtedly sell and prices would plummet as word spread of new black neighbors. It was an economic appeal that took advantage of whatever uncertainty white property owners felt about the demographic changes taking place. Even liberals who espoused integration had trouble standing up to the economic pressure to sell out.

In order to expedite the turnover of homes, some brokers took extra steps. "Real estate agents frequently hired African American subagents and other individuals to walk or drive through changing areas soliciting business and otherwise behaving in such a manner as to provoke and exaggerate white fears," according to the *Encyclopedia of Chicago*.

The buyers of the homes were often speculators, who would get them at cheaper and cheaper prices from frantic sellers. Then the speculators would resell them at greatly inflated prices to black families.

"Working virtually, if not covertly, in tandem, "respectable" real-estate agents flocked to do business in transitional areas once they had been broken by the maverick blockbusters. The net result was a gold-rush effect that destabilized residential communities as it maximized racial tensions and fears," according to the Encyclopedia of Chicago[8].

It was a feeding frenzy for real estate agents and speculators.

Some of the speculators who bought up houses sold them to black households on the installment plan. This was called "contract selling," and it was presented as a way to help black families gain homeownership at a time when discrimination in the provision of mortgage loans was very common.

It was often the only path to ownership a family could find, which gave the sellers the power to charge exorbitant fees for this form of credit. It was so costly that a high percentage of buyers ended up in default. When that happened, the seller could repossess the home, and sell it again. A family that had made payments and lost their home was at the seller's mercy.

Poverty & despair

Housing discrimination and economic exploitation of black housing consumers was only part of the picture of anger and despair in the ghettos. The other part was grinding poverty.

Many of the black migrants were not well educated and had no job experience outside of farming. When the incoming population of job seekers kept going up and the number of jobs peaked and started to shrink, poverty became even more damaging than racial segregation.

The condition of the poor black people of Detroit was described well by Kenneth Stahl in his powerful book, *The Great Rebellion*.

> The poor look out into a different world, through a prism that reflects only poverty, turbulence and despair. They live in a constant state of want for the things they know they will never have. Impoverished youth...conceal a hundred different agonies. With opportunity lacking, the mood of the ghetto is poisonous and self-destructive. The seeds of despair take hold of the very young, drain

them of their enthusiasm and replace it with fatalism. The poor do not look at life in terms of days, weeks or years but rather from a survivalist view of hours or minutes because they view their long-term future as nonexistent.

Manufacturing jobs began to be lost to global competition and increasing automation. Employers began to move to the suburbs, and getting to those suddenly remote locations was difficult for inner city residents. Black unemployment rose dramatically.

In 1968, a survey of 23 cities found that blacks earned less than whites in every one of those cities, averaging barely 70 percent of white income. They were more than twice as likely as the whites in those cities to be living in poverty.[9]

Whites fly, cities falter

As cities faced increasing social and financial challenges, middle class white households packed up their cars and moving vans and left for new suburban communities, the places that were made accessible by billions of dollars in federal spending on highway construction in the '50s and '60s.

As they left, the cities lost a very important source of tax revenue. That led to cuts in services, reduced investment in community facilities and a general need to increase taxes. Those changes caused still more people to move out of the cities.

Data on the shifts in population along racial lines from a government report includes the following:

- From 1962 to 1966, the white population of central cities declined by 1.3 million instead of rising 3.6 million as it would have if it had grown at the same rate as the entire white population.[10]
- In our ten largest cities, the black population increased by 1.8 million, or 58 percent, from 1952 to 1960. The white population in those cities declined by 1.5 million in the same period.
- Seventy-eight percent of white population growth between 1950 and 1966 took place in the suburbs. Ninety-six percent of the population in suburban areas was white at the end of that period.

CHAPTER THREE

Segregation as Government Policy

There are books, dramas, and documentaries that show how the U.S. government pushed southern states to let black Americans vote and attend the same schools as whites in the 1950s and '60s. The government wants to get these uplifting stories out to as wide an audience as possible.

What the federal government does not want to talk about is how it used tax dollars to encourage segregation in housing. From the 1930s until well into the 1960s, federal spending to build housing, redevelop cities and insure mortgages for home purchases helped private real estate interests and local governments continue the general practice of housing segregation.

Federal resources played an important role in keeping black families stuck in overcrowded ghettos while white families had nearly exclusive access to new suburbs with nice streets, good services, quality schools, and easy access to growing job centers.

The real estate industry as a whole treated racial segregation of housing as a prudent business practice on the grounds that mixing races would reduce property values. The federal government has provided mortgage insurance through the Federal Housing Administration (FHA) since the 1930s, and followed that line of reasoning until well into the 1960s. It generally would not insure loans on new housing developments unless they were restricted to white occupancy. It would not insure individual loans to buy existing homes unless the home was in a segregated area.

The FHA's policies were the dominant force in the booming housing industry. During the 1960s, the agency insured mortgages with a total outstanding loan amount of $6 to $7 billion per year.

Of 300 large subdivisions built from 1935 to 1947 in Queens, Nassau, and Westchester counties in New York, 83 percent had racially restrictive deeds, with preambles like this: "Whereas the Federal Housing Administration requires that the existing mortgages on the said premises be subject and subordinated to the said [racial] restrictions...[except for] domestic servants of a different race domiciled with an owner or tenant..."[11]

The federal government was determined to prevent school integration as well. Whole neighborhoods could be deemed ineligible for mortgage guarantees because, as the FHA underwriting manual stated, where children "are compelled to attend school where the majority or a goodly number of the pupils represent a far lower level of society or an incompatible racial element, the neighborhood under consideration will prove far less stable and desirable than if this condition did not exist."[12]

The '50s and '60s were the era of gigantic housing developments, and most of the biggest were supported by state and local governments in some way despite being for whites only. In many cases, cities provided land for the biggest projects by using eminent domain to buy up properties owned by or occupied by minorities and force them to leave.

For example, the city of New York facilitated the demolition of tenement houses on 72 acres on Manhattan's Lower East Side in the 1940s, displacing an estimated 10,000 people. The demolition made way for development of more than 8,700 apartments by Metropolitan Life, a place to be called Stuyvesant Town. The community's racial composition would be all white. "Negroes and whites don't mix," was the short explanation offered by Met Life Chair Frederick Ecker.[13]

Urban renewal

The federal Urban Renewal program helped cities to acquire land in areas perceived to be "blighted," demolish the homes and businesses in the area, and then transfer the cleared land at little or no cost to private developers for new development. The resulting projects often involved demolition of low cost housing to make room for construction of hotels, office buildings, arenas, stadiums, and roadways.

The program often ended up facilitating the demolition of block after block of older, lower-cost homes and businesses occupied by or owned by blacks who had very little input, if any, input into the process. Many people were forced to sell out for less than their properties were worth. What's worse, the cleared land that used to be a thriving if rundown community often sat empty for years while city officials worked out deals for new development.

In the 1940s and 1950s, San Francisco's Fillmore district was a thriving neighborhood with a mix of races and income groups. A person walking through the area west of downtown would have heard jazz from nightclubs that attracted great performers like Ella Fitzgerald and smelled the fresh barbecue from the local restaurants. There was a mix of people, but a majority of residents were black.

The Fillmore was declared blighted and suitable for redevelopment in 1948. The first demolition project began in 1956. The second phase began in 1964 and expanded the area to 60 square blocks. Eminent domain was used to purchase Victorian homes and buy out local businesses. The thriving black business community of nightclubs, barbershops, banks and retail stores was destroyed. Much of the land cleared was left vacant for decades as planning for major new commercial developments faltered.

In Pittsburgh, Pa., an entire neighborhood was torn down and replaced by the Civic Arena, displacing 8,000 residents, most of whom were poor and black.[14]

It was a pattern that was repeated all over the country.

• • •

The Urban Renewal Program had many problems, including the fact that citizens were rarely involved in planning what would become of an area through redevelopment. But the biggest failure was the destruction of tens of thousands of units of low-cost housing without providing for their replacement.

"Without adequate housing for the poor, critics will rightly condemn urban renewal as a land-grab for the rich and a heartless push-out for the poor and nonwhites," said Justin Herman, who ran the redevelopment agency for the city of San Francisco.

The harsh reality of how federal urban renewal spending affected black areas was summarized very well in a photograph from the Kercheval neighborhood in Detroit. In the foreground, there's a beat-up old house standing by itself in a desolate block. Looming up in the background are modern high-rise buildings.

It's a place where, in the '60s, the locals could not miss the stark contrast between the new buildings that came from urban renewal and the old, falling down housing that was home to many blacks. Every day, they were reminded that not only were the new build- ings mainly for the benefit of whites, but black families had been displaced in order for them to be built.[15]

Novelist James Baldwin talked about meeting a teenager from San Francisco who said he felt like an outcast in his own country because the city was tearing down his family home under its urban renewal program. "Urban renewal means moving Negroes out. It means Negro removal," he wrote. The term still resonates today with black people who had first-hand experience with the program in cities all over America.

Highway projects often had a similar impact on lower-income areas. In many places, they were constructed by demolishing older, often lower-income communities.

In the early 1970s, the city of Boston wanted to extend I-95 to downtown through the community of Jamaica Plain, dividing the community in half. Local activists organized protests and convinced the city and state to spare their community. However, it still took the community decades to recover, since demolition of existing buildings had already started. In 1995, a consortium of community groups, including the Jamaica Plain Neighborhood Development Corporation, Urban Edge and the Hyde Square Task Force, began planning for new development, including affordable housing with social services provided on-site.

• • •

A 1968 U.S. government report gave a picture of how the num- ber of units demolished for urban renewal and highway projects usually vastly exceeded the number of new units produced with gov- ernment help.[16]

In Detroit, a maximum of 758 low-income housing units were constructed with federal housing programs from 1956 to 1967. From 1960 to 1967, about 8,000 low-income units were demolished.

In Newark, from 1959 to 1967, a maximum of 3,760 low-income housing units were assisted. During the same period, more than 12,000 units, mostly for low-income families, were demolished.

In New Haven, Conn., from 1952 to 1967, 951 low-income housing units were created with federal help. From 1956 to 1967, about 6,500 housing units, mostly low-income, were demolished.

Perils of public housing

The main program used to provide low-rent apartments for poor Americans in the '50s and '60s was the public housing program, in which the federal government financed development of properties controlled by locally appointed public housing authorities.

"The whole theory behind public housing is that the individual is affected greatly by his environment and not only does the person develop more fully if he is given better surroundings but society benefits because a better citizen is produced," said Robert Weaver, head of the U.S. Housing Administration in the 1950s.

But local housing authorities were in charge of choosing locations and designs for the low-rent apartment buildings in their towns, and they were under the control of mayors.

Weaver worried that this local control by politically-appointed housing authorities would result in racial segregation and unequal treatment of blacks. He was right.

Despite the best efforts of Weaver and others in Washington, "local housing authorities sought to use housing development to create segregation where it had not previously existed." Within a short time, "public housing (occupancy) was overwhelmingly African American.[17]"

The pattern for segregation of the nation's public housing was set soon after the program began in the 1930s, as local authorities chose to make properties either all-white or all-black. Even returning veterans who were black could not find homes in white buildings.

In Chicago, the housing authority took a progressive approach for the late 1940s. It wanted to let black soldiers returning from World War II live in an apartment building called Airport Homes. The white residents refused to allow it, attacking potential black tenants with rocks and racial epithets. Thousands of people gathered outside the development to block the black vets from moving in.

Chicago Mayor Edward Kelly came out in support of integrated housing, saying, "All law abiding citizens may be assured of their right to live peaceably anywhere in Chicago."

That was the end of Kelly's political career. The Democratic Party replaced him as candidate for mayor in 1947, and their new choice, Martin Kennelly, proceeded to oversee construction of "the nation's most segregated city,"[18]

The problems with public housing went much deeper than turning away black families from individual properties. Much of the public housing that was meant to help people live better lives ended up becoming slum housing.

Some would say the public housing program became just another way for white institutions to create more ghettos. A more charitable critic might say the program's good intentions went badly wrong. In either case, it's a sad historical fact that tens of thousands of families and children suffered terribly from the squalid and dangerous conditions that were allowed to exist at many projects.

The tragedy of America's public housing can be traced to an urban design concept that was popular at the time. The idea was that, by building 10-, 15-, or even 20-story buildings, there would be plenty of room for open space between buildings. This often also involved building on so-called "super blocks," where the normal grid of streets and blocks was interrupted.

It also happened that clustering high-rises in this manner was the cheapest way to build large quantities of housing. It was also a way to isolate residents of all-black public housing projects from the surrounding neighborhoods.

• • •

Weaver, King and others argued for construction of small and mid-sized buildings in various locations throughout the cities, so that poor residents would not be concentrated in a small number of buildings. In most cities, they lost that argument. The fact that it would have used federal resources to encourage integrated neighborhoods was the clear, if unstated, reason that it was not pursued in most cities.

In Washington, public housing was never popular. From the beginning, conservatives fought the program on the grounds that it was a socialist idea that had no place in America. To get Congress to approve funding to continue the program in 1949, the Democratic administration of Harry Truman had to agree that the feds would not force suburban governments to accept construction of public housing within their borders.

After several years running the public housing operation from Washington and trying to talk sense to local housing authorities, Weaver's hopes had been pretty well dashed. He said public housing had become "a mechanism for the entrenchment of segregation at an unprecedented scale."[19]

Once again, Chicago distinguished itself for having the biggest problem with housing and the racial conflict that it embodied.

Richard Daley ran Chicago with an iron hand from 1955 to 1976, and preserved and advanced the cause of segregation. He concentrated public housing towers on the South Side. To ensure that whites and blacks remained separate, "Daley built a ten-lane interstate highway to cordon off the projects."[20]

Despite Weaver's objections, the city had created "the largest black ghetto in the nation." As Weaver and others had forecast, the results were disastrous for the city and the public housing residents, who lived in "rapidly deteriorating communities besieged by crime, social problems and failed management."[21]

The bad design, cheap construction and the failure to provide social services led to all kinds of problems, including high rates of crime. Even the police would not patrol some of the most dangerous projects.

One of those projects, the Robert Taylor Homes, completed in 1962, was named for an African American who chaired the board of the Chicago Housing Authority (CHA). Taylor had resigned from his post when the city council refused to endorse potential building locations throughout the city of Chicago that would encourage racially integrated housing.

Fast forward to the 2000s: The Robert Taylor Homes, along with many other high-rise projects, became so decayed and dangerous that the city began demolishing them and replacing them with smaller-scale properties.

By 1962, the Public Housing Administration had completed 500,000 units of public housing. More than 2 million people lived in the housing, more than half of them children.

As the '60s progressed, public housing became predominantly black and very low-income. A toxic combination of high poverty, bad design, lack of social services and ineffective management turned many projects into hellholes of crime and dysfunction.

Suburbs over cities

While federal funding was supporting the development of segregated public housing that often turned into slums, it was also helping
build and populate the overwhelmingly white suburbs. There was
a huge disparity between help provided for city dwellers and the
financial support that went to suburban households.

As of 1968, federal programs had not provided much housing for
the disadvantaged. In the 31-year history of subsidized federal housing, only about 800,000 units had been constructed, with production
averaging about 50,000 units a year in the early 1960s.

By comparison, over a period only three years longer, FHA insurance guarantees made possible the construction of over ten million middle and upper-income units.[22]

From the founding of FHA right through the 1960s, only a very
small percentage of new homes that were purchased using FHA-
insured mortgage were sold to African Americans. The racial composition of the FHA clientele has changed dramatically in recent
years, but the patterns of the earlier era were fundamental in establishing the racial composition of most American suburbs.[23]

CHAPTER FOUR

Planting Seeds of Change

While Martin Luther King, Jr., was taking it to the streets and confronting violent segregationists in Chicago, housing and urban issues were rising to the top of the political agenda in Washington, D.C.

At the Housing and Home Finance Administration, Robert Weaver was working to end segregation in federal housing and urban programs. Robert F. Kennedy was getting settled into his job as the U.S. senator for New York State. Lyndon Johnson was working to outmaneuver the many opponents of his bold ideas for how to save the cities and end housing discrimination.

Weaver would be at the center of the changes that were about to come, as he had been for much of his adult life. The Washington, D.C., native started a long career in government as part of the group that helped President Franklin Roosevelt implement the New Deal programs that eased the economic pain of the Great Depression.

Weaver helped the politicians who believed in integration to brave the political risks of putting those beliefs into action. Then he helped persuade white politicians who were skeptical about integration to support it anyway.

Weaver played three roles. He was an advocate, helping found and lead the National Committee Against Discrimination in Housing (NCDH). The organization produced hard-hitting research papers, including one titled "How the Federal Government Builds Ghettos."

He was also an administrator supervising hundreds of federal bureaucrats, some of whom did not support integration. Finally he was an advisor to presidents and members of Congress.

He was one of the very few black men who commanded the respect of the white power structure of Washington. What's more, his persistence in making well-reasoned arguments for integrated housing had a very important impact.

In 1961, President John F. Kennedy appointed Weaver to be administrator of the Housing and Home Finance Agency. That made Weaver the man in charge of Federal Housing Administration mortgage insurance used by millions to buy homes, construction of public housing, and reshaping American cities through the Urban Renewal program.

Weaver argued behind the scenes that Kennedy should take action to prohibit racial discrimination in federal housing programs, including the Federal Housing Administration's mortgage insurance programs. Kennedy hesitated for quite a few months, since he knew it would be met with strong objections.

Finally, on Nov. 20, 1962, the president signed Executive Order 11063, which prohibited federally funded housing agencies from denying housing or funding for housing to anyone based on their race, color, creed or national origin. It was a fundamental step forward for advocates of open housing. However, it was slow to yield results because of the entrenched bias in the real estate industry and the tendency of federal employees to enable that behavior regardless of the new policy.

Kennedy also proposed creation of a cabinet-level agency focused on the problems of America's cities and housing. But this required Congressional approval. Kennedy made several efforts to get that consent but failed. He probably would have tried again if he had not been assassinated in November 1963.

Johnson takes charge

Lyndon Johnson was vice president under Kennedy and served out his term. On May 22, 1964, President Johnson said it was not enough for America to be wealthy and powerful. He called on Americans to strive to create a "great society," one that would "end poverty and racial injustice." That November, with that promise ringing in the minds of a hopeful nation, he won election to his first full term as president by a landslide.

In his 1965 inaugural address, Johnson said that the essence of what makes America great is our constant quest to better ourselves and our nation. He said we are a "seeking nation," united in the quest for freedom and justice for all. The essence of the American character is "the excitement of becoming – always becoming, trying, probing, falling, resting, and trying again – but always trying and always gaining."

Johnson had the energy and the political mandate to get the liberal agenda for the cities and housing moving again and to follow through on the fight against housing segregation in federal programs as well as the private housing market.

Suddenly, the path toward creation of an urban agency was clear. The Housing and Urban Development Act was passed in the spring of 1965. The new Department of Housing and Urban Development (HUD) would come into being 60 days after Johnson signed the bill into law in September.

After struggling over who should lead the new department, Johnson named Weaver to be secretary of HUD in January 1966. Weaver became the first black man to serve as a cabinet secretary.

The victory in creating a cabinet level urban agency, which incorporated all the programs of the previous sub-cabinet level Housing and Home Finance Agency, came amid a bare-knuckle brawl over domestic programs.

Johnson had declared a War on Poverty, and it stirred up enormous controversy. Politicians on the right said it was a waste of money. Those on the left said it was not ambitious enough.

It's hard to imagine it today, but many powerful voices argued forcefully for a massive commitment of federal resources to eliminate slums and lift people out of poverty. The leader of the United Autoworkers was Walter Reuther, and his advocacy went far beyond the core issue of good wages and working conditions for the people assembling cars in the still-booming Motor City.

Reuther warned that conditions in the inner cities were intolerable and called for a federal Marshall Plan to fix them. He was talking about doing for our own cities what we did to rebuild Europe after World War II, a plan that was named after George Marshall, the secretary of state at the time. For reference, the $13 billion spent on helping Europe would be equivalent to $148 billion in today's dollars.

Reuther was a tenacious and outspoken advocate for civil rights and federal spending to alleviate poverty and urban decline. In 1966, Reuther criticized Johnson for not asking Congress for more money for federal poverty programs and fighting harder to overcome opposition. He warned that unless bolder action was taken, poor people would "search for answers in the blindness of night, and reason will yield to riots and brotherhood will yield to bloodshed, and we will tear asunder the fabric of our society."

Reuther's criticism of Johnson for not doing enough had strong support in the U.S. Senate.

For much of 1966 and 1967, the condition of our cities and the best ways to help them was a hot topic in Congress. Sen. Abraham Ribicoff of Connecticut chaired the Senate Subcommittee on Government Operations, and used it to pick apart the policies of the Johnson administration and the operation of the new urban agency, HUD.

He held 33 hearings and heard from 100 witnesses, from cabinet secretaries to homebuilders.

Sen. Robert Kennedy joined Ribicoff in his hearings and was also critical of the level of spending on HUD programs. He believed more needed to be done to empower inner city residents to start their own business ventures and create jobs under their control.

Sen. Paul Douglas, a Democrat from Illinois and an ardent supporter of civil rights, chaired a congressional commission on urban problems, which held hearings in 16 cities between May and October 1967. It became a forum for attacking Johnson's programs.

Ribicoff introduced a number of bills, including one that would eliminate all substandard housing in all urban areas of the nation. He figured it would cost $1 trillion and take 12 years to fully "rehabilitate" the cities.[24] Those numbers were not well received in the White House or the Congress. But the urgency expressed by the two senators would soon appear to have been well justified.

A 'model' program for cities

Johnson and his advisors had high hopes for HUD. They wanted the new agency to do more than just finance housing, sewers and redevelopment of slums. They wanted it to coordinate a comprehensive approach to the problems of the urban poor.

They hit upon the idea for something called the Model Cities Program. The idea was to combat urban poverty with comprehensive plans combining physical renovation and rebuilding with social programs. HUD was to be at the center, working with cities and helping them coordinate assistance from a rapidly increasing variety of federal programs.

It was the "big idea" that liberals hoped would lead to major progress in as many as 150 cities.

The law authorizing the program came to a vote in November 1966, but passage did not come without some heavy compromises.

The program was very controversial because it would give HUD power to coordinate various federal programs and tell local governments what they could and could not do. It did not sit well with Republicans, and Paul Fino (R-N.Y.) was their primary spokesperson.[25]

He claimed that the program could be used by HUD to require suburbs to accept public housing, and be taxed to pay for "slum schools." He warned that forced busing and redistricting of schools would be used to achieve racial integration of suburban schools.

To get the program approved, Johnson had to accept an amendment saying it could not be used to promote racial balance in schools. It was a very large concession to the wishes of suburban voters and a disturbing indication that comprehensive approaches would not come easily, then or now.

Johnson wanted funding of $1 billion per year to launch the program. Reuther and others said this was far less than was needed. But Congress disagreed. It provided about half that, or about $450 million per year. The program was also handicapped by the weakening of the original mechanisms envisioned to give HUD real authority over programs run by other departments. As a result, the goal of coordinating programs such as job training along with housing development was not readily achievable.

Meanwhile, the voices that wanted to do less instead of more were also growing as 1966 progressed. Gerald Ford, the Republican leader of the House of Representatives at the time, set the tone, saying:

> How long are we going to abdicate law and order in favor of a soft social theory that the man who heaves a brick through your window or tosses a firebomb into your car is simply the misunderstood and underprivileged product of a broken home?

Other Republicans moved in to pick apart the specifics of HUD's programs and how it managed them.

There were certainly inefficiencies in some of the new programs- Model Cities was particularly challenging, since there were conflicts to be resolved between departments and procedures to be ironed out. Plus, the stated goal of trying to involve local clients of the pro-

grams in decision-making was a completely new idea – a practice for
which federal bureaucrats were completely unprepared.

The fact that the program had received much less funding than
was requested also undermined the goal of implementing comprehensive solutions.

Some said that Model Cities was the greatest domestic policy
failure of Johnson's presidency. But it appears now that the program was doomed by the very high expectations put upon it at a
time of great stress, as well as a lack of agreement on how to evaluate its results.

It was also a classic example of the Catch 22 that keeps resur-
facing throughout HUD's history: The president who is in power
asks Congress to appropriate enough money for a program to have
a measurable impact, Congress cuts the appropriation dramatically,
then the program is criticized and attacked for not having a sufficient measurable impact.

That shortfall in results then becomes a political justification to
end that program.

Model Cities only lasted about eight years, but it established
some very important principles. Chief among them was that troubled neighborhoods required more than construction of apartments
and commercial spaces but a comprehensive approach that included
social services and community engagement, especially youth programs. Another key lesson was to involve citizens in deciding how to
use federal resources, to empower them to shape their own future.
That alone was a huge step forward from the days when federal officials and big-city mayors reshaped the cities with no regard at all
for the impact on the poor.

A detailed analysis of the impact of the program is beyond the
scope of this book. However, stories and photographs from some of
the cities where Model Cities operated give us a glimpse of happy
inner city youth engaged in constructive activities. In Baltimore, for
one example, photos from the late 1960s tell a story of a program
that helped give inner city kids new opportunities to learn and contribute to society, important alternatives to life on the streets.[26]

Weaver and his fledgling cabinet agency also took charge of the
Urban Renewal Program, which was generally hated by black urban
dwellers and loved by commercial real estate interests and mayors.

The 1965 law that created HUD called for a change in the program's direction. It still financed demolition of buildings to make

way for major commercial projects, but a new idea was introduced: Maybe we could rehabilitate and repair some of the older housing in our inner cities rather than bulldozing it into dust. Maybe displacement of some of the poor families living in urban renewal areas could be avoided.

It sounds obvious today, but it was a major change in the thinking of the time and a major step forward for how the federal government addressed slum conditions.

Congress and the rats

The first sign that the War on Poverty might not end in victory came in the fall of 1966. The Democrats lost 47 seats in the House and three in the Senate. Ronald Reagan was elected governor of California. In 1967, the new Congress went on the attack against Johnson's programs. In one very telling example, Johnson proposed an appropriation of $40 million for rat extermination in urban areas. This was a grave concern for ghetto residents, since poor sanitation services in ghettos had allowed rats to breed, and poor maintenance of apartment buildings had left tenants at the mercy of the pests. Black children suffered an extraordinary number of rat bites.

Republicans and Democrats alike made fun of the proposal as a liberal boondoggle. One legislator reportedly joked that Congress should just buy a bunch of cats and deliver them to the cities. The appropriation was not approved.

The 1965 law also opened up a new era in how the federal government provided rental housing for poor Americans.

A new alternative to public housing was created. The Sec. 236 program provided funds for construction of privately owned housing that would be leased to poor people under a contract between the private owner and the federal government. It was hoped that private real estate developers could do a better job creating decent housing without increasing racial segregation.

HUD also began to offer low-income tenants the option of using government subsidies to pay rent for housing in existing buildings. This was a major innovation because poor families who received subsidies could use them to rent where they wished to live.

In theory, this gave them much more mobility, and the potential to live outside of segregated areas.

Meanwhile, Weaver was also making steady progress in getting HUD and FHA staff, and private real estate players to follow Kennedy's order banning housing discrimination.

CHAPTER FIVE

Violence Shocks the Nation

Martin Luther King Jr., smiled broadly as he watched President Johnson sign the Voting Rights Act in a grand ceremony on August 6, 1965. Less than a week later, he and other leaders of the civil rights movement were stunned by terrible news out of Los Angeles.

LA was known for Hollywood movies and surfer music. The Beach Boys had just released "California Girls." But to many black residents, the city was known for a militarized and racially biased police force. It was known for a strict if unwritten code about where black people could live or visit. If a police officer spotted a black person in an area where he or she was not supposed to be, it would not go well for that person. LA Mayor Sam Yorty was harshly dismissive of any criticism of the police.

While southern blacks were gaining voting rights, California's black population was still smarting from an assault on their rights and dignity – from the voters of the Golden State. The California legislature had passed a law outlawing discrimination in housing. But the state's real estate brokers put a referendum on the 1964 ballot to repeal the law. The voters approved it by a two to one margin.[27] The message was clear. The voters of California would not be told they had to rent or sell housing to black people.

It was against that background that a simple traffic stop on a hot August day triggered five days of rioting in the city's Watts district in south central LA.

A California highway patrolman arrested a young black man for drunken driving. When the young man's family members objected to the arrest, they were arrested, too. The incident triggered an outpouring of anger and resentment that could not be tamped down by community leaders who called for calm.

Looting began, then fires were set, and before long, there was shooting. The National Guard was mobilized. Television screens and newspapers all over America were filled with images of soldiers patrolling the streets with bayonets mounted. This is how the commission appointed to make sense of the riot described what went down:

> Thursday through Saturday, perhaps as many as 10,000 Negroes took to the streets in marauding bands. They looted stores, set fires, beat up white passersby whom they hauled from stopped cars, many of which were turned upside down and burned, exchanged shots with law enforcement officers, and stoned and shot at firemen. The rioters seemed to have been caught up in an insensate rage of destruction. By Friday, the disorder spread to adjoining areas, and ultimately, an area covering 46.5 square miles was affected...
>
> When the spasm passed, thirty-four persons were dead, and the wounded and hurt numbered 1,032 more.[28]

It has been estimated that the loss of property attributable to the riots was over $296 million in 2015 dollars (adjusted for inflation). Burning and looting damaged more than 600 buildings. One-third of those were totally destroyed by fire.

The Watts riot shocked millions of Americans who had been confident that race relations were improving in the North, and evoked a new mood in the ghettoes around the country.

Over the next two summers, the country would find out just how much the mood had changed, and how much anger had built up in the minority communities in many cities, mostly in the North.

• • •

One year later, it was Chicago's turn to burn. On a hot July day on the west side, the police shut off a fire hydrant people were using to cool down. Someone turned it back on again and was arrested. A crowd gathered. Windows were broken and firebombs were thrown at buildings. The governor called in 4,200 national guardsmen to help restore order.

On the night of July 14, six policemen were shot along with an uncounted number of civilians, as the city police fought rioters, according to news accounts. The Chicago Transit Authority shut down bus and elevated lines, and police blocked off main streets. In one violent incident, more than 100 policemen exchanged shots in an hour-long encounter with snipers in two high-rise buildings at Lake and Wood Streets.[29]

When it was over, three black people had been killed by stray bullets, among them a 13-year old boy and a 14-year-old girl. Over 500 people had been arrested.

The events were recounted by journalist Ellis Close, who lived in the area:

> I did not seek out the '60s; they found me: in my living room where, as a kid during a hot summer night, I bore witness to the madness of the times. That madness took the form of a massive police assault unfolding outside two buildings just across the way. As my parents, my brothers and sisters and I sat huddled away from the windows, listening in horror to the gunshots and screams, I knew that something huge was happening outside and that the world I thought I knew was about to change.[30]

The next eruption took place in Cleveland, Ohio. An area on the near east side known as Hough had gone from 95 percent white to 74 percent black in a very short time. Poverty and unemployment were high. The housing was decayed and decrepit, with mostly absentee landlords. Families displaced by land clearance for giant urban renewal project had squeezed into the housing available to blacks in Hough. Severe overcrowding resulted.

Less than a week after the Chicago riot, a white bar owner in Hough posted a sign saying that he would not serve blacks. When that resulted in an argument, a crowd gathered and the city police responded. An even bigger crowd gathered. There were four nights of violence. Fires were set, stores were looted, and Ohio National Guardsman patrolled the area in jeeps.

Four people were killed. On the fourth night, Sam Winchester, a 54-year-old black man, was killed while walking to a bus stop. While he lay dying, Winchester told police that he had been shot by whites who targeted him from a passing vehicle.

Forty-three disorders and riots were reported during 1966, according to the U.S. government.

The new year of 1967 started peacefully enough. The first Super Bowl was held in Los Angeles. Tens of thousands of people gathered for a "Human Be-in" in San Francisco's Golden Gate Park.

It was the beginning of the counterculture of rock music and psychedelic drugs. Timothy Leary, the advocate for experimentation with LSD, coined the catch phrase that would define the mood of the mostly white movement: "Turn on, tune in, drop out."

Over the spring, thousands of young people found their way to the city by the bay for what would be called the summer of love. The movement got its anthem in May of that year, when Scott McKenzie released the song "San Francisco (Be Sure to Wear Flowers in Your Hair)."

Summer of hate

Back east, the mood and the living conditions could not have been more different. For black residents of the ghettoes in Detroit, Newark and other cities, it was shaping up to be the summer of hate.

The first sign that it would be a very bad summer came in June, when rioting broke out in Tampa, Florida.

The living conditions give important insight into why black residents were angry. Six of every 10 houses inhabited by blacks were unsound. Many were shacks with broken windows, gas leaks and rat holes in the walls. Most black kids never reached the eighth grade. Less than 5 percent of black high school seniors attained the minimum passing score on the state's college entrance exam.

On Monday, June 12, before order had been restored in Tampa, trouble erupted in Cincinnati, Ohio, after police shot a young black man. At first, the rioters broke some windows but did not loot or start fires. But the next evening, fires were being set, cars were being stoned, and windows were being broken. The National Guard was called into the city.

In Newark, N.J., conflict had been brewing for some time over a proposed urban renewal project. The plan was to clear over 150 acres of land in the city's Central Ward for a state medical college. The project would displace thousands of black families living in the area.

Newark had 400,000 residents in 1967, but in the previous 7 years, 70,000 white residents had moved out of the city. The city's new majority was mostly black but also Latino. However, white officials still held political control.

Tensions built day by day over that summer. Then in July, a

rally was held to protest police brutality in front of a precinct station house. Rocks were thrown at police. As news of the disturbance spread, people poured into the streets. In short order, looting, gunshots and fires were being reported in a widening area.

The National Guard was mobilized and by early afternoon, it had set up 137 roadblocks.

Twenty-three people were killed in Newark, including two children. *Life* magazine called it "a shooting war in the streets" and "a predictable insurrection."

The violence was intense. In one case, a large contingent of National Guard troops and New Jersey state troopers converged on the Rev. William P. Hayes Homes.

"At 6 p.m., two columns of guardsmen and state troopers were directing mass fire at Hayes Homes in response to what they believed were snipers. On the tenth floor, Eloise Spellman, the mother of several children, fell, a bullet through her neck."[31]

Three women watching the scene from various locations nearby suddenly found themselves under fire from the guardsmen. All three women died. The gunfire appeared to be in response to bottles thrown from the upper floors of the nearby buildings.

The riot lasted from July 12 to 17. When it was over in Newark, 23 people had been killed.

The historical record is not clear about how much sniping actually took place, or how two public safety personnel were killed. What is established in the official U.S. government report on the incident is that the New Jersey National Guard and state police fired 13,326 rounds of ammunition in three days in Newark.[32]

· · ·

Twelfth Street in Detroit was renamed Rosa Parks Blvd. years ago, but long-time residents of the motor city will never forget what happened there in 1967, a few days after Newark had calmed down. Some say it was the beginning of the end for the city's days of prosperity.

Two black soldiers had returned from Vietnam that summer, and on July 22, a group of their friends gathered to celebrate. The men returned to a city that had seen its black population grow from 30 percent to 40 percent of the total population in seven years. Over 10 years, enrollment in city schools had gone up by 50,000, resulting in severe classroom crowding. Fifty-seven percent of the students were black. The high school drop out rate was over 50 percent.

In the 12th street neighborhood of the inner city, 30 percent of black men under 25 were unemployed.[33]

Some 60,000 poor people were crammed into the neighborhood's 460 acres, living in squalor in subdivided apartments. The Detroit Police Department, which had only about 50 African Americans at the time, was viewed as a white occupying army. The only other whites seen in the neighborhood commuted from the suburbs to run their stores on 12th Street.[34]

The "welcome home" party took place in an unlicensed after hours night club, the kind of place the police raided with regularity. When they arrived on the night of this party, they decided to take all 85 patrons into custody. While they waited for vans to arrive to haul people off to jail, a crowd gathered.

An hour passed before the last prisoner was taken away. By then, about 200 onlookers lined the street. A bottle crashed into the street. The remaining police ignored it, but more bottles were thrown. The police began to leave the area, hoping the crowd would disperse on its own once they were gone.

What happened next was described in *The Great Rebellion*, by Kenneth Stahl:

> As the police began to breathe a premature sigh of relief, some- one from the crowd picked up a bottle and launched it high into the air. Like the home crowd at a football game watching a last chance 'hail Mary' pass, the mob bridled as the bottle arced past a streetlight, began its descent and crashed right through the rear window of the last police cruiser, which wisely kept on going. Like scoring the winning touchdown with time running out, the crowd went berserk. The crowd surged down 12th Street, doing a dance of destruction as they went.

For a time, the police were ordered to contain the trouble without firing any shots, to avoid aggravating the rioters. As many as 10,000 people filled the streets, some taking part and some watching.

The riot spread from 12th Street to the entire west side and later, to the east side, encompassing most of the central city. As the looting subsided, armed men began firing at police from windows. News reports about how many snipers there were or how many shots they fired vary widely.

Around 6:30 a.m., the first fire broke out, and soon much of 12th street was ablaze. By midmorning, every policeman and fireman in Detroit was called to duty. Firemen were attacked as they tried to battle the flames.

The long, hot summer

The riots of the 1965 to 1967 period were investigated and document thoroughly by several commissions and committees appointed by governors and the U.S. Congress. There were cover stories in magazines and newspapers. But even after reading all the details, it's hard to comprehend what it must have been like.

The riots almost always happened during the hottest days of summer, when poor people without air conditioning often had trouble sleeping. They usually started at night.

The photos and recollections of those who were there tell a story of four groups of people:

- The rioters, who sometimes reveled in acts of violence that some described as their way to take revenge on white society and individual storekeepers they felt had ripped them off or disrespected them personally.

- The older, more restrained black residents of the affected areas who tried to promote peace, some of whom owned property they wished to protect. To a large extent, rioters spared businesses owned by blacks.

- The white store owners who rushed to defend their stores with shotguns and other weapons.

- The bystanders of all races in the cities with the worst rioting, who listened closely to radios buzzing with reports of violence and watched smoke rising over their cities. Many of them left town, at least temporarily.

When it became clear that the Michigan National Guard could not restore order, President Johnson ordered the U.S. Army's 82nd Airborne Division to enter the city.

The riot lasted five days, and resulted in 43 deaths, 1,189 injuries and over 7,200 arrests. More than 2,000 buildings were destroyed.

A tally of the unrest and damage for 1967 was taken by The Senate Committee on Government Operations. In 75 disturbances in

67 cities, there had been 83 deaths. The committee said that disorders defined as "serious" or "major" took place on 41 occasions in 39 cities.

The worst violence was in Newark and Detroit. Other cities where people died in riots that summer: Cincinnati, Jackson, Miss., Milwaukee, New York City, Plainfield, N. J., Erie, Pa., Houston, Pontiac, Mich., and Rochester, N.Y.

After the riots of 1965 to 1967, politicians, police chiefs, mayors and civic leaders all asked the same question: What could be done to make sure that such terrible upheavals did not happen again?

On July 29, 1967, while the fires in Detroit were still smoldering, President Johnson appointed a commission to look at the causes of the riots and what should be done to address the problems that they had exposed.

The National Advisory Commission on Civil Disorders was headed by Otto Kerner, the Democratic governor of Illinois. The commission would work quickly to find out why the riots happened, and what could be done to prevent them. It interviewed or surveyed thousands of people, including some who had engaged in rioting. It was a remarkably in-depth study of housing, urban, and racial issues in America.

When the commission came out with its findings and recommendations, they would shock the political world of Washington almost as much as the riots did.

CHAPTER SIX

Progress & Reversal

Hope was in the air on New Year's Day, 1968. Memories of the shocking violence that had erupted in 1967 were still fresh, but Americans had tremendous confidence in our country's ability to solve problems.

We figured that if we could put a man on the moon, as we were close to doing at that time, we could solve the problems of the cities and make progress toward racial understanding.

Steady progress was being made in the fight for equal housing opportunity. The city of Louisville, Ky., was among the states and localities that had passed laws prohibiting racial discrimination in housing. In Louisville, especially, it was a signal victory for nonviolent organizing and voter registration to have finally elected enough leaders who opposed segregation and supported such a law.

However, the fragile political alliance of liberal northern Democrats, progressive Republicans, labor leaders, and civil rights advocates who were working for more federal assistance for cities was about to be tested. At the same time, tension was growing between civil rights leaders who favored nonviolent protests and those who favored aggressive tactics and the idea of "black power."

There had been no shortage of dire warnings about what would happen if the federal government did not act aggressively to address the problems of the cities and do more effective battle against segregation.

For the previous two years, there had been hearing after hearing that left little doubt about the severity of the problems, the cost of trying to fix them and the potentially even higher cost of not fixing them.

The most important findings and recommendation came from

the Kerner Commission. It released its report on Feb. 29, 1968, four months before the due date. The detail and depth of the report was remarkable, and Americans were eager to read it.

"Our nation is moving toward two societies, one black, one white – separate and unequal," the commission said. "Segregation and poverty have created in the racial ghetto a destructive environment totally unknown to most white Americans," it added.

The commission did not stop there. "What white Americans have never fully understood – but what the Negro can never forget – is that white society is deeply implicated in the ghetto. White institutions created it, white institutions maintain it, and white society condones it." The report said that blacks living in the ghettos viewed police, in general, as agents of white power and repression.

The panel called for massive new public spending to help address the problems of the inner cities.

The official report was made available through the usual government channels, but that was not sufficient to meet the demand from Americans to know what was wrong and what needed to be done. Bantam published it as a paperback book, and 1.6 million Americans went to their local bookstores to buy it. Millions more read about it in newspapers. It was discussed in every newspaper and on every radio and TV news show. Marlon Brando even read from the report on a popular television talk show.

Spinning out of control

The report sparked vigorous debate about the cities and race relations. But that spring, events began to spin out of control rapidly as the need for social progress ran head-on into the painful reality of the escalating war in Vietnam.

King had become more confrontational in his relationship with the president. He was organizing a massive march on Washington to fight poverty among people of all races and had begun to demand an end to the war. There were increasing political divisions in Washington and more anti-war protests across the nation.

On March 31, Johnson announced he would not run for re-election.

On April 3, King went to Memphis for the second time to help support black sanitation workers who were striking for better wages and working conditions. On the afternoon of April 4, he was shot to death at the Lorraine Motel.

News accounts of the time describe the gatherings of grieving men and women in the black ghettos of America. They quote people in the streets who saw King's death as one more example of how white society was killing black people. The news accounts suggested that many felt there was little reason to keep hoping that change could be obtained through nonviolent protest.

The reaction in cities across the nation varied. Where white leaders who were trusted engaged people that night, there was peace. In Indianapolis, for instance, Sen. Robert Kennedy followed through with a previously scheduled speech in the inner city. He made a passionate plea for peace, and asked the mostly black audience members to pray for our country:

> What we need in the United States is not division; what we need in the United States is not hatred; what we need in the United States is not violence or lawlessness, but love and wisdom, and compassion toward one another, and a feeling of justice towards those who still suffer within our country, whether they be white or whether they be black.[35]

The mayor of New York City was John Lindsay, a member of the now-vanished breed of socially progressive Republicans. He had been the vice chairman of the Kerner Commission, and the strongest advocate for its strong condemnation of white racism.

As the streets of Harlem, the black ghetto of Manhattan, filled with angry people, he rushed to 125th Street and began to walk and talk with the people there. He expressed his sorrow and repeated his oft-stated concern for social progress. There was no rioting despite the highly charged atmosphere.[36]

In Washington, D.C., President Johnson went on television to ask Americans to remain peaceful and continue working toward equality. He called in civil rights leaders from around the country for a meeting at the White House the next morning at which he urged them to try to maintain peace in the black community.

In Virginia, at the Pentagon, the domestic military operations center created after the 1967 riots roared into action. The brass there worked into the night to draw up detailed plans for deploying the Army or Marines if things got too violent for state National Guard units.

On the night of King's murder, angry crowds gathered at

14th and U Streets, N.W., just 1.5 miles north of the White House. Stokely Carmichael was head of the militant Student Nonviolent Coordinating Committee (SNCC), which had offices nearby. SNCC had always been more radical than King's Southern Christian Leadership Conference, and its leaders were much more prone to talk about civil rights in militant terms.

On the night of King's death, Carmichael visited stores along 14th Street and demanded that the owners close out of respect for King. Other black leaders urged the crowd to stay calm and avoid violence, but it was not enough.

The young men on 14th Street started smashing windows and looting. Fires were set. As midnight neared, a heavy rain began to fall and things calmed down, but it would not last.

The next day, Friday, April 5, teenagers began to walk out of classes at inner city schools. At roughly midday, the fire department started to get calls about fires, one after another.

Everyone feared the worst was about to happen. City streets clogged with traffic as office workers tried to get out of town quickly. Traffic was so jammed that some people abandoned their cars and walked across the bridges to the northern Virginia suburbs.

Black smoke rising

Later, at the White House, Johnson was dining with close aides. Looking out the window to the east, past the Treasury building, the group could see smoke rising.

Johnson sent two aides out in an unmarked car to see first hand what was happening. When they returned with their report of a city in flames, he called out the U.S. Army's Third Infantry Regiment. The troops set up a machine gun nest at the center of the front entrance to the White House. Other federal troops stood guard at the Capitol.

By Wednesday, April 10, there were 15,530 Army and National Guard soldiers in and around Washington.

In the district, 510 businesses were shuttered after the riots, resulting in the loss of 5,000 jobs. A total of 2,115 people were displaced from their homes. Over 1,200 buildings had been burned.

Just a short drive to the north, in Baltimore, things got out of hand very quickly. The violence spread over 1,000 blocks. Store owners armed themselves with shotguns and rifles to defend their stores. That evening, U.S. Army troops were deployed to help quell the violence. At the peak on Tuesday morning, there were 11,570 troops in the city.

When it was over, the toll was six dead; more than 700 people injured; 5,500 arrested; 1,050 businesses looted, vandalized, or obliterated by fire; and an estimated $13.5 million in property damage (in 1968 dollars).

In Chicago, the rioting started late on April 5. Between 4 pm and 10 pm, there were 36 major fires, including an entire block on Madison Street. Rioters cut firehoses to prevent firefighters from putting out the fires. Reports said shots were fired at firefighters.

Rioting partially or completely destroyed 300 blocks. There were 575 fires and 3,273 people were arrested. By midnight Sunday, 11,709 army and National Guard troops were on duty in the city.

Some of the worst destruction occurred at Madison and Homan St, just 5 miles west of the Michigan Ave shopping district. The destruction was described in an article in the *Chicago Tribune* headlined "Madison St. a Blackened Scar in Heart of Chicago."

> In the block just east of Homan Ave, the torch of the arsonist had done its worst work. Hardly a building remained untouched. It was as if a flamethrower had played up and down the streets, burning roofs and crumpling walls until they arched inward to meet the heat-blackened, twisted steel structural members that hung into the ruins.

The article said rioting had raged uncontrolled in the area for 40 hours.

After a full week of violence, the last spasm of rioting took place in Kansas City. In most cities, the National Guard was withdrawn as soon as violence had subsided. However, in Wilmington, Del., the governor ordered the guard to stay deployed in the black ghetto. The occupation continued until a new governor took office over nine months later.

The toll of the violence that had affected over 100 cities: Thirty-nine people died, 2,600 were injured, and 21,000 arrested. There was damage of $65 million in 1968 dollars. Adjusted for inflation, it would be equivalent to $435 million today. [37]

Riots bad enough to require National Guard troops to be deployed occurred in Cincinnati, Detroit, Durham, N.C., Goldsboro,

N.C., Greenville, N.C., Jackson, Miss., Joliet, Ill., Kansas City, Memphis, Nashville, Pine Bluff, Ark., Pittsburgh, Pa., Raleigh, N.C., Tallahassee, Fla., Tuskegee, Ala., Wilmington, Del. Wilmington, N.C., Youngstown, Oh.

Regular U.S. Army troops were deployed to Baltimore, Chicago and Washington DC.

Entire sections of our major cities looked like war zones, with burned out buildings surrounded by piles of rubble, and empty buildings abandoned by owners fleeing the inner cities. The previously well-established migration of affluent whites from cities to suburbs picked up more steam.

For thousands of people who lost homes or businesses or loved ones, or who were wounded, the riots would not soon be forgotten. City officials and community groups would struggle to rebuild burned-out areas for decades. State and federal money for rebuilding did not come quickly, sometimes not for decades, and for some places it did not come at all.

Some politicians celebrated the idea that a race war had been avoided. Other observers knew that was not entirely true.

"A race war did in fact come to America that day, but it turned out to be a Cold War, not a hot one," wrote Clay Risen in *A Nation on Fire*.

"When the smoke cleared and the sirens ran down, an invisible wall went up between urban and suburban America every bit as real as the one in Berlin. Many would argue that it is still standing today."

Political reaction

The reaction to the riots split predictably along racial lines. Many white people believed that "a massive African-American conspiracy was behind the riots." according to Fred Harris, a U.S. senator from Oklahoma, and a member of the Kerner Commission. The black community, on the other hand, was irate about the overreaction of law enforcement personnel during the riots and resentful of the unwillingness of public officials to focus on the underlying causes of the disorders, Harris wrote.

Fear and distrust between the races had been part of everyday life in northern cities for decades, but in 1968, the divisions started to look more like battle lines. Black militants talked about revolution, and young black men on the street no longer had a national role model for the nonviolent approach to social change. White politicians talked increasingly about getting tough on crime and increasing the capacity of police to shut down civil unrest.

The presidential campaign season got underway very soon after the Kerner Commission issued its report. Sen. Robert Kennedy (D-N.Y.), the brother of the late President John F. Kennedy, announced his candidacy in March.

As a senator, Kennedy had shown time and again that he cared deeply about black Americans and the problems of the poor residents of the ghettos. He was impatient with Johnson's policies, saying they did not go far enough to improve urban conditions. In announcing his candidacy in a speech at the University of Kansas, he summarized the state of the nation after the riots and the Kerner report.

> ...millions of citizens are looking for their answers, [they are looking] to force and repression and private gun stocks – so that we confront our fellow citizen across impossible barriers of hostility and mistrust...I don't believe that we have to accept that. I don't believe that it's necessary in the United States of America. I think that we can work together – I don't think that we have to shoot at each other, to beat each other, to curse each other and criticize each other. I think that we can do better in this country. And that is why I run for president of the United States....
>
> I have seen the people of the black ghetto, listening to ever greater promises of equality and of justice, as they sit in the same decaying schools and huddled in the same filthy rooms – without heat - warding off the cold and warding off the rats. If we believe that we, as Americans, are bound together by a common concern for each other, then an urgent national priority is upon us. We must begin to end the disgrace of this other America.[38]

On June 4, 1968, when he won the California presidential primary, Kennedy became the front-runner for the Democratic nomination.

Blacks and Mexicans in California had voted in record numbers, and they were overwhelmingly for Kennedy.[39] As one of Kennedy's advisors reportedly told him after this remarkable showing, "Bob, you're the only white man in the country they trust."

At the Ambassador Hotel that evening, Kennedy talked about his ideas for creating jobs in the ghettos. Later, speaking to his joyful supporters, he talked about healing the divisions that were tearing our nation apart. As he left the podium, he was shot at point blank range. He died the next morning at the age of 42.

It was the end of "the murderous spring of 1968," as author Jack Newfield called it. It was also the end of hope for hundreds of thousand of eager young people who longed for peace on the streets and overseas. The belief that the future would be better than the past died with King and Kennedy, Newfield wrote.

"We had already glimpsed the most compassionate leaders our country could produce and they had all been assassinated," he wrote.

Meanwhile, back in the central cities of America, the flight of whites accelerated.

Whites who had left the cities in the '50s and early '60s still viewed downtown areas as places to shop and go for entertainment. After 1968, that changed. Even people who worked in downtown areas left at quitting time and did not return until the next workday or work week. Weekend shopping trips to large downtown department stores were a thing of the past. In many places, suburbanites stopped indulging in nights out at downtown restaurants or theaters.

The exodus of blacks from the South was now matched by the exodus of whites from northern cities. Relatively affluent black households worked even harder to overcome racial discrimination and move out of central cities. This left the median incomes and property tax bases in central cities areas even lower than they were before.

In Washington, D.C., it's estimated that the white population decreased by one percent per year from 1969 to 1994.[40]

"People poured out of Baltimore, especially whites. The incipient urban depopulation that occurred between 1950 and 1960 ...snowballed after the riots. From 1970 to 1980, Baltimore's population declined from 906,000 to 787,000."[41]

The exodus dramatically affected commerce, as large downtown department stores gradually disappeared. They were superseded by suburban malls that opened in the 1970s and 1980s.

It was the same story all over America as malls sprouted throughout suburbia like spring flowers.

The backlash begins

As whites fled the cities, there was a concerted political movement to blame the riots on black militants and civil rights leaders who had been influenced by Communist organizers.

Sam Yorty had been the mayor of Los Angeles when the Watts riots started and became a national advocate for getting tough on social unrest. He insisted there was no validity to any protest against police brutality, and that anyone saying otherwise was probably representing Communist "agitators." He argued for stronger law enforcement and tougher laws to prevent a recurrence of urban violence.

The California legislature turned Yorty down when he asked for a law that would let police arrest anyone who appeared to be getting ready to "incite a riot."

Yorty kept up his advocacy as a candidate for the California governorship and the presidency. He did not win either office. However, millions of Americans and dozens of other politicians shared his views.

From 1968 on, many cities and states would resolve to spend much more on preparing law enforcement for the threat of what they described as urban "guerilla warfare" and training national guard troops to control riots.

The militarization of the police was about to get underway in earnest. Likewise, the political justification for police to practice racial profiling had been established tacitly if not explicitly in many people's minds.

With King and Kennedy dead, and Johnson retired, no one fought very hard for implementation of the Kerner Commission's "prescription for life," as King had called its recommendations.

No one paid much attention to the disturbing warning that Kerner left for future generations about what would happen if its prescription was not filled:

The rising concentration of impoverished Negroes and other minorities within the urban ghettos will constantly expand public expenditures for welfare, law-enforcement, unemployment, and other existing programs without reversing the tendency of older city neighborhoods toward decay and the breeding of frustration and discontent.

But the most significant item on the balance of accounts will remain largely invisible and incalculable – the toll in human values taken by continued poverty, segregation, and inequality of opportunity.[42]

The Slippery Slope of Stalled Progress

CHAPTER SEVEN

Urban Decay Redux

In the 1960s, people of color who wanted to buy homes had to contend with artificially inflated prices, an extremely limited choice of areas where they were permitted to buy, and the brutal exploitation of "contract selling." In the 2000s, they were victimized by another wave of exploitation known as predatory lending.

In communities of color, predatory lenders circled like sharks, and they found plenty of victims. These private lenders, who were generally not connected to any government housing programs, deliberately targeted communities of color to peddle loans with very risky features, like adjustable rates and artificially low "teaser" rates. These lenders knowingly encouraged many people to take out loans even though the borrowers had little chance of repaying them.

Lower-income communities made substantial progress in the 1990s as the economy grew and government programs were reasonably well funded. But the predatory lending surge turned back the clock. It led to huge increases in the number of people who defaulted on their mortgages. Home prices dropped, mortgage payments went up, and a death spiral hit housing markets.

Foreclosure filings were made on 14.2 million properties from 2008 through 2014, according to RealtyTrac. Owners of many of those homes lost them in completed foreclosures, some were still headed toward that outcome, and others kept their homes but faced ongoing struggle to stay current on their mortgages[1]

Losing it all

For households that lost their homes to foreclosure, the financial impact was devastating. Many of the victims had all their savings tied up in the form of equity in their home and lost it all. Many of them had to move into apartment rentals. Some former homeowners even became homeless.

Many victims of predatory lending used the high-risk loans to refinance homes they had already owned for some time, often free of any debt. For those households, what had been a stable financial situation turned upside down overnight.

The foreclosure crisis hit predominantly black and Hispanic areas especially hard. Data shows that unscrupulous lenders targeted these areas for the highest-risk, highest-cost types of mortgage loans, such as adjustable-rate mortgages and loans with high prepayment penalties.[2]

This led to higher-than-average default rates within the Hispanic and African American communities, according to the Bipartisan Policy Center, which brought together Republican and Democratic government officials and experts on housing in 2014. The center's housing panel said many of the families had good credit, decent incomes, and everything else necessary to qualify for traditional long-term, fixed-rate loans.

Despite that fact, they were not offered those kinds of loans. They were "steered into exotic and costly mortgages they did not fully understand and could not afford," the commission said.[3]

This "deliberate targeting of minority areas for the sale of risky and expensive loans," as the commission described it, continued to have an impact every day in inner cities and lower-income towns across America long after the press declared the housing crisis to be over.

African American and Hispanic borrowers were almost twice as likely to have lost their homes to foreclosure as whites, according to the Center for Responsible Lending (CRL), a nonprofit, nonpartisan organization based in North Carolina that works to protect homeownership and family wealth by fighting predatory lending practices.

Differences in income and credit history did not explain why communities of color were hit harder, CRL said.[4] For example, the foreclosure rate for low- and moderate-income African Americans was about 80 percent higher than that for comparable white households. Foreclosure rates for higher-income Latinos were more than three times that of higher-income whites. African-Americans and Hispanics with good credit received high-cost loans more than three times as often as white borrowers, CRL said.

"Communities of color got the worst of everything. They were given the highest-risk, most expensive mortgages, they received the worst servicing from their mortgage lenders, and they have suffered the most damage from the nation's long economic slump," said Liz Ryan Murray, policy director for National People's Action, a Chicago-based group that has been fighting against discriminatory home lending practices since the 1970s.

One study of mortgage data from Baltimore, Md., found that "race and neighborhood racial segregation are critical factors explaining black disadvantage across successive stages in the process of lending and foreclosure, controlling for differences in borrower credit scores, income, occupancy status, and loan-to-value ratios."[5] Translation: Black and Hispanic borrowers got treated worse than whites at every step in the process, even when they had the same credit scores and loan characteristics.

Sociologists refer to the foreclosures in minority areas as one of the "processes of cumulative disadvantage" that continue to undermine black socioeconomic status in the United States today. In other words, the cycle of predatory lending followed by foreclosure and disinvestment is just the latest example of how people of color continue to lose out time and again in the housing market.

Bush thinks big

President George W. Bush was right when, in 2002, he called for increasing homeownership as a way to help minorities build wealth and move up the economic ladder. In 2005, he issued a presidential proclamation saying:

A home provides children with a safe environment in which to grow and learn. A home is also a tangible asset that provides owners with borrowing power and allows our citizens to build wealth that they can pass on to their children and grandchildren. The benefits of homeownership extend to our communities. Families who own their own homes have a strong interest in maintaining the value of their investments, the safety of their neighborhoods, and the quality of their schools. Homeownership is also a bedrock of the American economy, helping to increase jobs, boost demand for goods and services, and build prosperity. [6]

The president set a goal to increase the number of minority home-owners by 5.5 million families by the end of the decade. It was a grand vision, one that working class Americans were eager to embrace.

People of color began to hope that they could stretch their finances just enough to buy homes and build equity as home prices rose.

Killing the dream

The decline in homeownership among people of color doesn't get much press attention. This is partly because defenders of the banking industry blamed the foreclosure crisis on the government for encouraging more mortgage lending to less affluent minorities.

These organizations never mentioned President Bush or his aggressive homeownership push. Instead, they focused their attacks on Democratic presidents who were out of office many years before the foreclosure crisis broke in the latter part of Bush's time in office.

It's true that the federal government has worked since the 1970s to reverse the longstanding discrimination in the lending process. In the 1960s, banks routinely denied credit to African Americans and to neighborhoods that were undergoing racial change. This process was called redlining, because bankers used to draw big red lines on the maps in their offices to show where they were refusing to make loans.

Landmark legislation was passed to encourage banks to make credit available to all borrowers in their service areas. Bush and other leaders wanted to go even further to encourage homeown-ership but made some bad miscalculations along the way.

Bush's mistake was to unleash private lenders to offer risky loan products as home prices rose, and then sell them to investors as part of mortgage-backed securities. Many people, including at-torneys general in many states, warned that this was a recipe for disaster. They were ignored.

Then, making things worse for minorities, the federal government overreacted to the crisis and curtailed the flow of mortgage credit to all potential home buyers, especially to less-affluent families who did not have the savings to make large down payments. Private lenders became much more conservative. The result was the denial of mort-gage credit to hundreds of thousands of aspiring homebuyers.

They would not be subject to their landlord's decisions about rent increases or the extent of upkeep or repairs. They could have a yard for their kids and a front porch to enjoy the evenings.

Bush backed up his words by pushing Congress to provide new subsidies to help lower-income people cover the downpayments required to buy homes. He proposed a program in which the Federal Housing Administration would have insured mortgages without any downpayment requirement for first-time buyers.

Some of the president's initiatives may have worked well, but they were overwhelmed by the flood of predatory lending and the foreclosures that it caused. The positive vision of a large increase in ownership and wealth among minorities ended as a nightmare, with millions of families confronting the cruel mathematics of not being able to make their mortgage payments.

There are enough statistics about lending and foreclosure patterns to choke a mortgage broker, but to see the bottom line, look at the trend in the rate of homeownership.

Black and Hispanic families have always had a lower rate of homeownership than whites. They are far more likely than whites to be renters, which means that they enjoy fewer tax breaks than whites and have less chance than whites to build equity from the appreciation of home values.

The tragedy is that during the 1990s and into the early 2000s, before the foreclosure crisis, the rate of homeownership was increasing for everyone, including people of color. In 1994, the rate of homeownership was 42.1 percent for blacks, 40.3 percent for Hispanics, and 69.8 percent for whites. The white rate exceeded the black rate by 27.7 percentage points.

The rate of ownership peaked for black households at 49.7 percent in the spring of 2004. The rate peaked for Hispanics at 60.6 percent in fall 2006.

White households' rate stayed at a high of about 76 percent for most of 2005 and 2006. That's when the housing bubble started to deflate and foreclosures started to climb.

In the first quarter of 2015, the rate of homeownership had fallen to 42 percent for blacks, a decline of 16 percent. The rate for Hispanic households dropped to 44 percent, a 28 percent decline. For white households, the homeownership rate was 72 percent in 2015, a reduction of only 5.5 percent from its peak.

The 30-point differential between the white and black homeownership rates in 2015 was the widest gap since statistics have been kept. That gap says a great deal about the future trends in economic inequality in America, since home equity is one of the primary ways that families build wealth.

The declining rate of black and Hispanic homeownership tells only part of the story of the disparate impact of the foreclosure crisis. Millions of families still owned their homes after the foreclosure crisis but have struggled every month to keep them.

A homeowner is described as being "underwater" when they owe more on their mortgage than their home is worth on the market. The technical term is negative equity, but being underwater is apt slang because families in that position feel like they are drowning under the pressure of their mortgage debt.

More than 9.8 million American households were still underwater on their mortgages as of December 31, 2013, according to Zillow, the online real estate information service. That's close to one-fifth of all mortgaged homes in America.

Drowning in debt

Nationwide, about 27 percent of homeowners in minority areas had negative equity compared to about 15 percent of owners in white areas, according to "The State of the Nation's Housing 2014," from the Harvard Joint Center for Housing Studies (JCHS).

Many of those troubled homeowners are still locked into predatory adjustable rate loans with interest rates that will increase, putting them at continual risk of eventually defaulting on their mortgages and facing foreclosure.

For a case in point, consider Ferguson, Mo., where protests raged in 2014 and 2015 over the killing of an unarmed black man by a white police officer.

In the zip code that includes Ferguson, 49 percent of homes were "underwater" at the end of 2013, according to "Underwater America," from the Haas Institute for a Fair and Inclusive Society, at the University of California, Berkeley.

That means that every second house you see in Ferguson has a market value that is less than what the owners owe on their mortgage. That means they have very little chance of ever selling the house for a price that would let them pay off their loan. If they did sell, every penny of the sales price would go to the mortgage holder, and that still would not be enough. The owners would still be in debt even after selling what is, for most of them, their only major financial asset.

New American slums

The negative impact of foreclosures went beyond the immediate loss of the money affected families had invested in their homes. It aggravated the blight that already existed in many poor, inner city neighborhoods and triggered new decay in towns and inner suburbs that had been doing well.

Facing foreclosure or the struggle with negative equity, many property owners just walked away from their homes, seeing no benefit in continuing to keep up property tax payments and maintenance work. As foreclosures increased, the number of vacant, crumbling homes steadily increased.

It hurt the economic prospects of entire neighborhoods and towns by leaving a wake of abandoned and vandalized homes in lower-income and minority areas.

Several cities in California, including Stockton and San Bernardino, declared bankruptcy partly because of the economic ripple effect of declining property tax revenue and increased expenses to deal with urban blight.

• • •

Overall, the number of vacant properties across the country increased 51 percent, from nearly 7 million in 2000 to 10 million in April 2010.[7] This excludes properties with seasonal occupancy.

Ten states saw increases of 70 percent or more, according to the Census Bureau. Analysts believe this is due primarily to the foreclosure crisis. In 2012, there were some 4,700 neighborhoods across the country where more than 1 in 5 homes were vacant.[8]

Vacant homes often deteriorate drastically. In hard-hit areas, they can become havens for squatters, prostitutes, or drug dealers. These areas are the new American slums—blocks, neighborhoods, and even entire towns full of shattered dreams, broken windows, weed-choked yards, caving roofs, and pervasive crime.

The decay discouraged any new investment in commercial or residential projects, and even basic upkeep of houses owned by people who were not underwater. No one wants to put money into an area that appears to be in decline.

The chain reaction of price declines, foreclosures, and disinvestment has meant declining property values for everyone in those areas, including people who were current on their loans or owned their homes free and clear.

Home values dropped 26 percent between 2006 and 2013 in neighborhoods that were predominantly minority—more than three times the decline in neighborhoods that were predominantly white, according to JCHS, which puts out an annual report titled "State of the Nation's Housing." This report is considered the most comprehensive analysis of U.S. housing conditions.

Zombies are a major contributor the decline in neighborhoods – that is, zombie foreclosures.

That is what "fair credit" advocates call it when a bank starts to foreclose on a family, throwing it into turmoil, but does not complete the legal process in a timely way. In many states, it can take a year or two in the best case, and if the lender is understaffed or drags its heels, the delay can stretch out for several years.

Lenders that hold the mortgage on a property generally want to wait to take ownership until they see potential to resell the property on the open market. If there is no such potential, they like to start the foreclosure process, drive the owners who defaulted on their loan out of the property, and then sit on it until they see economic potential in taking ownership.

Many lenders who foreclose do nothing to maintain the buildings or the lots on which they sit. Sometimes they don't even bother to board up the windows or cut the grass. You can imagine the impact that has on a neighborhood.

• • •

In Cook County, Ill., in 2013, there were more than 11,700 zombie properties where a foreclosure proceeding had not been resolved for more than three years, according to The Woodstock Institute. "Because neither the borrower nor the loan servicer has clear control of the property, neither has a strong incentive to assume responsibility for the property. Zombie properties, therefore, are likely to be poorly maintained or blighted, which threatens the stability of surrounding communities," Woodstock said.[9]

In the most distressed neighborhoods of Baltimore, Chicago, Cleveland, and Detroit, about 60 percent of vacant units have been held off market, indicating they are in poor condition and likely a source of blight, JCHS added.

In Pittsburgh, 27 percent of single-family homes were vacant in 2013. The city had 35,000 real estate parcels that were delinquent on property taxes.

Lower-income areas have little prospect for home prices to recover soon. That means their problems will continue for years because there's not much potential for any lender to recoup the cost of fixing up and selling properties in these areas.

"In some communities with many foreclosed properties, the crisis threatens to doom the entire neighborhood to a cycle of disinvestment and decay. A cluster of vacant properties can destabilize a block. A cluster of troubled blocks can destabilize a neighborhood. The costs are substantial," according to Chicago's Business and Professional People for the Public Interest.

Many cities affected by large numbers of foreclosures can't pick up the slack left by negligent owners and lenders. Wrestling with budget shortfalls themselves, they can't afford to fix up properties that are falling apart or clean up trash- and weed-filled yards.

Tough luck for buyers

One of the less obvious consequences of the foreclosure crisis was the damage it did to the political support for government programs that help lower-income people of color become homeowners.

Private lenders tightened up on their standards for making loans, and the government did not do enough to encourage continued lending to people who wanted to buy homes in areas where values had declined.

The reduction in availability of credit was an extreme reaction, because, when it's done right, with counseling and careful underwriting of long-term, fixed-rate loans, helping lower-income people buy homes works reasonably well.

Many of the nonprofit organizations that have established programs for such families came through the foreclosure crisis with fewer problem loans than commercial lenders out to make a profit.

"We've proven over almost 20 years of providing opportunity for low- and moderate-income people that the American dream of sustainable homeownership is alive and well," said Marietta Rodriguez, vice president of homeownership and lending programs at Neighbor-Works America.

Her organization works with a network of 235 local, community-based, nonprofit groups to deliver services and programs that help low-income people buy homes and stay in those homes.

The key to successful lending to less affluent people is extensive counseling, both before and after they buy a home. This approach, which almost all nonprofit housing groups use, focuses on getting potential borrowers to be realistic about their finances and the burdens of ownership. It helps them understand the full picture and make sure they have their financial affairs in order.

This patient approach to helping people realize the benefits of homeownership continues to be a very viable approach to achieving the economic benefits that President Bush envisioned in 2005.

CHAPTER EIGHT

The Persistence of Inequality

Conservative political factions would like you to believe that the problems described in the first part of this book are ancient history. They argue that most federal and state spending for housing and urban programs is no longer needed, if it ever was.

Don't believe the propaganda. The patterns and scope of our problems have changed, and old-school racial segregation has declined. However, segregation of American households by race and income still poses serious problems for our society, problems that are just as likely to worsen as improve in coming years. The concentration of poverty in central cities and close in suburbs still does terrible damage to families with young children every single day.

Four decades after the Fair Housing Act was passed, the degree of racial inequality had barely changed, according to Patrick Sharkey, an associate professor of sociology at New York University.

"The story of neighborhoods and race in America is one of enduring, inherited inequality. Despite the high hopes of the civil rights era...the stark racial inequality in American's neighborhoods that existed in the 1970s has been passed down to the current generation of African Americans," Sharkey wrote in his 2013 book, *Stuck in Place: Urban Neighborhoods and the End of Progress Toward Racial Equality*.[10]

The children who were raised in the most disadvantaged areas during the civil rights period are overwhelmingly likely to now raise their own children in remarkably similar environments. For the families living in today's ghettos, the challenges and risks associated with life in America's poorest neighborhoods represent a continuation of a family history of disadvantage.

Sharkey reported that over 70 percent of African Americans who lived in the poorest, most racially segregated areas in 2013 were from families that lived in similar places in the 1970s. This does not necessarily mean they stayed in the same communities where they were raised, but that they resided in places with similar socioeconomic characteristics.

The book describes how political decisions and social policies have led to disinvestment in black neighborhoods, persistent segregation, declining economic opportunities, and a growing link between African American communities and the criminal justice system. It says that some of the most persistent forms of racial inequality, such as gaps in income and students' test scores, can only be explained by considering the neighborhoods in which black and white families have lived over multiple generations.

The flip side of Sharkey's finding is that people who manage to leave areas of concentrated poverty can look forward to substantial improvements in their lives. In his book, he states that:

When families are able to move out of the most violent, poorest, racially segregated neighborhoods in the nation, their children's academic and cognitive test scores rise sharply ... and when the degree of concentrated disadvantage surrounding a family declines, children's economic fortunes improve substantially as they approach adulthood.

Sharkey's point about the importance of residential mobility is the very same principle that drove the progressive political leaders of the 1960s to work so hard for policies that would help poor families move out of the ghettos and into the suburbs of our metro areas.

Concentrated poverty

Poverty is not a good thing for anyone, but it does more damage if you are poor AND surrounded by other poor people. Academic research has shown that poor people who live in areas of concentrated poverty have more problems and greater levels of dysfunction than those who live in areas with a range of income groups.

From 1970 to 2010, the number of high-poverty neighborhoods in the U.S. tripled, and the number of poor persons living in them has doubled.[11] "High-poverty neighborhoods" are places where 30 percent or more of the population live below the poverty line.

The poverty line was an income of no more than $24,250 for a family of four in 2015. Anyone who's tried to support a family on that much income knows it's an extremely low cutoff point. If a more realistic definition were used, it would mean there were many more high-poverty areas.

Thirty-nine percent of the urban poor lived in such high-poverty neighborhoods in 2010, up from 28 percent in 1970.

"The burden of concentrated poverty is borne disproportionately by persons of color," according to "Lost in Place," a report from *Cityobservatory.org*. "In 2010, African-Americans were eight times more likely than white urban residents to live in high-poverty neighborhoods, and Latinos were five times more likely to live in these high-poverty neighborhoods," according to the report.[12]

"Arrested progress in the fight against poverty and residential segregation has helped concentrate many African-Americans in some of the least desirable housing in some of the lowest-resourced communities in America," according to "The Unfinished March", a 2013 report from the Economic Policy Institute (EPI).[13]

Forty-five percent of poor black children lived in neighborhoods with concentrated poverty between 2006 and 2010 on average, the report found. Only 12 percent of poor white children lived in such places during that time.

New York to Tokyo

The gap between poor areas and affluent ones was described very well in a 1997 article by Edward Glaeser, a professor of economics at Harvard.

He used the South Bronx to illustrate his point because this borough of New York City was the poster child for urban decay in the 1970s and 1980s. It was the place where presidential candidates routinely came to stand in front of cameras and express their concern about the blighted areas of our cities.

It made a good case study, partly because the decay was so vivid, but also because it is just a 30-minute subway ride from the glitzy hotels and luxury retail of the east side of Manhattan. A few more stops on the train and you're in the heart of American business on Wall Street.

In his article, Glaeser talked about the dire condition of areas with a "concentration of impoverished ethnic groups," saying:

These districts, commonly called "ghettos," function culturally, intellectually, and economically apart from the busy downtowns.

The distance from Wall Street to the South Bronx, along these dimensions, is greater than that between New York and London or Tokyo. Cities throughout history have contained distinct ethnic districts. But rarely have they been so isolated and impoverished as the African-American districts found in U.S. cities today.[14]

This was written in the late 1990s, after a solid period of economic growth in America.

The South Bronx has improved markedly since the article appeared, but it is still a radically different world from most parts of Manhattan, just as the forgotten ghettos of San Francisco and Chicago are from the bustling downtowns of those cities.

• • •

Living in an area of concentrated poverty is correlated with a host of social and economic challenges. Children in neighborhoods with concentrated poverty experience more social and behavioral problems, have lower test scores, and are more likely to be a victim of crime. The schools are often crowded and the drop-out rates are higher. Housing is expensive relative to the incomes of the people living in the area.

These "high poverty neighborhoods" are plagued by problems that are glaringly obvious when compared to "communities of opportunity," an informal term used to describe towns that have good schools, low crime, easy access to jobs, good municipal services and high median incomes.

The idea of living in such communities is something most low- and moderate-income families can only dream about because of the high cost of housing. But some go beyond dreaming in the hope of giving their kids a better life.

Some parents falsely claim to live in nearby towns that have good schools so that they can obtain a better education for their children by sending them to the nearby classrooms.

Recently, the suburban community of Glastonbury, Conn., kicked 48 students out of its schools because they lived in Hartford, and their parents lied about residency in order to get them into the high-quality suburban schools.

Glastonbury, is a town of 34,427. It is 93 percent white and has a median income of $80,660. It is located about 12 miles from the downtown of Hartford, a city of about $125,000, which is 30 percent white, and has a median income of just $27,753.

The situation illustrates the lack of access to affordable housing in most of Connecticut's cities, according to David Fink, policy director for the Partnership for Strong Communities, a Connecticut housing policy organization, writing in the *Hartford Courant*. Fink said only 31 of the state's 169 municipalities have affordable housing. Those areas where the poor can afford to live have overburdened schools, fewer enrichment classes, and fewer resources like parks, children's programs, and library branches, all of which help kids do better in school.

Apartheid American Style

Douglas Massey and Nancy Denton wrote the book on continued segregation in America in 1998. They called their book *American Apartheid: Segregation and the Making of the Underclass*. The title refers to the rigid residential separation by race that was practiced in South Africa for many years. While South Africa abolished apartheid as official policy in the early 1990s, separation of the races had continued in America, the book pointed out.[15]

The book links persistent poverty among blacks in the United States to the "unparalleled degree of deliberate segregation" they experienced in American cities, despite efforts to enforce the Fair Housing Act of 1968. "Segregation is perpetuated today through an interlocking set of individual actions, institutional practices, and governmental policies," it said. "In some urban areas, the degree of black segregation is so intense, and occurs in so many dimensions simultaneously, it amounts to 'hyper segregation.'"

Under conditions of extreme segregation, any increase in the overall rate of black poverty yields a marked increase in the geographic concentration of indigence and the deterioration of social and economic conditions in black communities, Massey and Denton wrote.

In more recent research, Massey and others report that there have been reductions in racial segregation. However, the general progress slowed to a crawl and may have reversed after the Great Recession began.

In addition, levels of segregation and isolation are much higher and the declines considerably slower among large metropolitan areas with large black populations, according to a paper co-authored by Massey, one of the few academics who specializes in this topic.[16]

The segregation index is the statistical tool sociologists use to measure the residential separation of the races. It translates the data about how many members of a racial group live in each neighborhood to come up with a single number for each American city. The number indicates how many households in the racial group being studied would have to move so that their neighborhood would have the same proportions of each race as the city as a whole.

This index declined in the 1990s and 2000s in almost every metropolitan area with a population of 500,000 or more. However, the index was still over 50 percent for 70 of the 102 cities on that list in 2010.[17]

Even the most segregated American cities have seen steady progress toward less racial separation, but that progress has been slow.[18]

However, the statistics on segregation are hard to interpret. It's a complex subject, and there are many ways to look at the data, some of which have more to do with the political bias of the group that funded the research than any claim to better methodology.

Mapping segregation

If you want to know how segregated your city or town was in 2010, you need only fire up your computer. The data is available in a remarkably detailed and user-friendly way courtesy of the *New York Times*. The paper used census data to create an interactive map of the entire U.S. down to the level of census tract. Color-coded dots show the exact racial composition block by block. Go to www.projects.nytimes.com/census/2010/map

However, Glaeser from Harvard made an important observation about the decline in the segregation index in his 1997 paper. He referred to the fact that in the 1960s, ghettos existed primarily because legal restrictions made it impossible for blacks to leave. Talking about the situation in the '90s, he wrote:

> The barriers today are more subtle, and economic....Middle-class blacks can buy their way out of the ghetto, but those at the bottom of the income ladder are unable to leave. The black segregation index declined primarily because areas that used to be all white now have a small number of blacks. The African-American ghettos have not

become any less black. They just house a smaller share of the nation's urban black population.[19]

Other analysts have pointed out that the movement of higher-income blacks has actually made the poverty that always existed in the ghettos even more concentrated.

Two professors from the University of Wisconsin–Milwaukee gave us a more understandable measurement of segregation in 2003. They looked at the racial composition of our communities on a block-by-block basis. They used data for all 8.2 million blocks in the United States from the 2000 U.S. Census. They found that much of the United States remained racially segregated, with almost a third of the African American population living on blocks that are more than 90 percent black and over half of the white population living on blocks that are more than 90 percent white.

The researchers said the data shows the need for remedial efforts to combat racial discrimination and racial steering in housing; to support affirmative housing opportunities, particularly for low- and moderate-income African American families interested in moving into suburban areas; and to provide public and private support for integrated and diversified neighborhoods. [20]

The statistics on school segregation echo the data on housing segregation. They too show how things have changed for the better,

America's most segregated cities in 2010

1. Detroit, black-white dissimilarity score of 79.6.
2. Milwaukee, 79.6
3. New York City, 79.1
4. Newark-Union, N.J., 78
5. Chicago, 75.9
6. Philadelphia, 73.7
7. Miami, 73.0
8. Cleveland, 72.6
9. St. Louis, 70.6
10. Nassau-Suffolk (Long Island), N.Y., 69.2

Note: The dissimilarity score is a different name for the segregation index.
Source: The Persistence of Segregation in the Metropolis: New Findings from the 2010 Census

but only to a fairly modest degree, and that progress has slowed or reversed recently.

The percentage of black students in intensely segregated minority schools in 2011 was highest in the northeast, where 51 percent of students attended such schools. This was about the same percentage as in 2001. It was an increase from 42 percent in 1968. In other regions, the 2011 percentage varied from 34 percent to 43 percent.

Except for the northeast, the 2011 rates were all down from the 1960s, but the rate of decline has decreased substantially. In the south the percentage was still down from the '60s, but it has increased steadily from its low point in the 1980s.[21]

The bottom line is that progress toward more integrated schools appears to have stopped. One report attributes this to a decline in the number of "desegregation plans" that school districts are operating under court supervision to comply with the historic Brown vs. Board of Education decision that outlawed discrimination in the educational system.

"Promoting school integration is important because—now as a half century ago—segregated schools are unequal schools. The more nonwhite students a school has, the fewer resources it has," according to the Economic Policy Institute

Poverty and Unemployment

Black poverty, as with poverty overall, declined dramatically through the 1960s, falling from a rate of 55.1 percent in 1959 to 32.2 percent in 1969. That was a bit more than three times the poverty rate for whites at the time. Since then, however, progress in reducing black poverty has been agonizingly slow and uneven.

The poverty rate among black households hit a low of 22.5 percent in 2000. The Great Recession drove the rate back up to 27.6 percent by 2011. The rate has declined only slightly since then, down to 27.2 percent in 2013.

By contrast, the poverty rate for whites was 9.6 percent in 2013. The black poverty rate was a bit less than three times the poverty rate for whites.

In 2013, the median income for black households was $34,598, about 41 percent less than the median white household income of $58,270, according to the Census Bureau.[22]

The median family for all black families in 1969 was $5,999, about 40 percent less than the median white family income of 9,794.[23]

Several authors have made much of the fact that recent trends show poverty is no longer just an urban and rural problem but is increasingly a problem in the suburbs. There's truth to this. Between 2000 and 2011, the poor population in suburbs grew by 64 percent—more than twice the rate of growth in cities (29 percent), according to "Confronting Suburban Poverty in America."[24]

However, the percentage of the population in poverty remained higher in urban areas. On a national basis, the urban poverty rate was 83 percent higher than the suburban rate (22 percent versus 12 percent, respectively).

In 2012, the black unemployment rate was 14.0 percent, 2.1 times the white unemployment rate (6.6 percent). From the 1960s to today, the black unemployment rate has consistently been about 2 to 2.5 times the white unemployment rate.

The average unemployment rate from 1963 to 2012 was 11.6 percent for blacks and 5.1 percent for whites, EPI stated.

Rich people in, poor out

In some places, lower-income households are moving to the suburbs and wealthier folks are moving from the suburbs into the cities.

The media likes to do stories about how some central city areas have been revitalized, taking advantage of historic buildings and natural amenities like waterfronts. Artists and entrepreneurs are celebrated as urban pioneers as they try to spark a revival in hard-hit parts of Detroit and other cities.

But the positive impact of this trend is highly exaggerated, partly for political reasons. It makes the general economic condition of our cities look better to investors and it reduces the ability of mayors to make a case for continued financial support from Congress.

Artists and other urban pioneers have been important catalysts for revitalization of inner cities. But real estate development and gentrification is like fire. It's good right up until it becomes destructive.

In some cities that offered large tax breaks for job creation and where large real estate developers sought profits from large-scale development, gentrification started to cross that line. It brought the higher-income residents that were necessary to attract crucial retail development like grocery stores. But it also made housing unaffordable.

Balancing the need for reinvestment and job creation versus the need to maintain housing affordability is very difficult.

In San Francisco's Mission District, this has led to serious economic distress as developers displace long-time residents to make way for construction of new, high-priced condos. Protesters are generating political support for rent control and possibly even a ban on new construction.

In Manhattan's Lower East Side, the battle against blight and decay went on for the better part of a century. Today, one could say that the results may have been too good. Now, instead of celebrating, residents are watching the few remaining low-cost apartments being converted to ultra-expensive apartments and multi-million-dollar condos. One of the only grocery stores in the area is being replaced by condos.

It's nothing new. When low-income people find themselves in an area that attracts high-income new arrivals, rents and real estate values rise, and the lower-income residents of the area almost always lose out.

It's not unlike the process of displacement that occurred under the federal urban renewal program in the 1950s and 1960s, which is still remembered as "Negro Removal." The federal government no longer routinely subsidizes projects that result in displacement. However, local governments tend to be less concerned. After all, property taxes are their financial mainstay, so they tend to place a higher priority on increasing property values than on avoiding displacement of lower-income people.

Some cities, like Boston and San Francisco, try to offset the impact by building low-rent housing, but it's very rare that the volume of replacement housing matches the amounts that are lost.

CHAPTER NINE

Segregation, 21st-Century Style

The shortage of affordable housing in America has reached crisis proportions. This crisis affects everyone up to and including the middle class. It affects people of all races and nationalities. But it hurts people of color the most. You might call it the 21st-century version of residential segregation.

In recent decades, housing costs have been rising faster than incomes for most Americans, and, after a brief pause during the recession, this "affordability gap" has been growing even wider.

The standard financial wisdom is that a household should budget 30 percent of its income for housing costs. In 2012, 50 percent of all American households who rent their homes paid more than 30 percent of income for rent, according to Harvard's Joint Center for Housing Studies (JCHS).

That is twice the percentage of "cost-burdened" households as there were in 1960, when only 24 percent of renter households paid more than 30 percent of their incomes for rent.

If you want to allow for a higher percentage of income to go for rent, that's fine. But even at a standard of 40 percent, one-third of all renters paid too much of their income for rent in 2013.

Back in the 1960s, the Census Bureau did not even report how many Americans paid more than 50 percent of their income for rent. It was a tiny number. But in 2013, one-quarter of all renter households in America paid more than half of their income after taxes to keep a roof over their head.[25]

The data shows that the range of people and areas affected by the affordability problem has increased. But the problem is most serious for people who have less income to start with, and who are on fixed incomes such as Social Security or other forms of assistance, or a small pension.

Among households earning less than $15,000 per year, an astounding 70 percent paid more than half their incomes for rent. That meant they had only $7,500 left for every other household expense—for a full year.

Rents rising, incomes stuck

Rents for apartments remained stable briefly during the recession but then quickly resumed their long upward trend.

April 2013 marked the 34th consecutive month of growth in rents as measured by the Consumer Price Index, according to JCHS. In its "The State of the Nation's Housing 2014" report, JCHS said rents were up 2.8 percent nationwide for 2013, about the same increase as in 2012.[26]

By three separate measurements applied by Harvard's JCHS, median rents have gone up as a percentage of income in most years since 1986, with the notable exception of years when the economy was in a recession.

Rents have jumped dramatically in many places. In Portland, Ore., for example, from late 2011 to late 2013, rents increased 7.1 percent, according to the Oregon Office of Economic Analysis. In cities like Boston and San Francisco, where employment has been strong, demand for housing is driving up rents even more quickly.

In its report "America's Rental Housing," Harvard's JCHS said the number of very-low-income renters is increasing while the supply of housing available to them is decreasing. In 2003, 16.3 million very-low-income renters competed for 12 million rental units that were both affordable and in adequate condition.

By 2009, the number of very-low-income renters rose to 18 million while the number of affordable, adequate, and available units dipped to 11.6 million, pushing the supply gap to 6.4 million units.

Income stagnation since the recession has not helped the situation.

The median annual household income dropped 7.2 percent from January 2000 to June 2013, according to an analysis of Census Bureau data by Sentier Research. As of June 2013, median household income was $52,098. The decline continued even after the economic recovery officially began in 2009, the researchers said.

It has been an "unprecedented period of economic stagnation," said Gordon Green of Sentier Research. The data shows that almost every demographic group was worse off in 2013 than it was in 2009, with the exception of households with householders 65 to 74 years old.

The declines in income have been larger than average for some groups, including black households.

The problem of poverty is especially damaging to children. In 2011, more than one-third of black children (38.8 percent) and Hispanic children (34.1 percent) were living in poverty. The poverty rate for families with children headed by single mothers hit 40.9 percent in 2011.

Adjusting to high costs

The main adaptation to the high cost of housing is to give up on the dream of living in a nice neighborhood with good schools and access to jobs, where crime is low and transportation is good. This lack of affordable options is a primary reason why people remain living in areas of concentrated poverty: it's where the cheap housing can be found, along with high crime and low-performing schools.

The good news is that severely dilapidated housing is no longer the problem it once was. Government data shows the percentage of households living in severely dilapidated housing has been decreasing steadily.

However, the improving conditions refer only to the structures involved, not the neighborhoods in which they are located. The government does not count how many Americans live in neighborhoods that are severely troubled by blight and crime. It's a major gap in the data, since the trade-off between finding something at a low rent and the conditions in which one has to live are extreme

Sometimes, it's as simple as taking a place near a noisy freeway or next to an oil refinery. In many cases, it's much more dangerous. The worst compromise is to move to a rundown neighborhood with a high crime rate in order to get an affordable rent. The price of this compromise can be enormous, especially for families with children.

In many inner-city neighborhoods, random gunfire is a regular occurrence, resulting in injuries and deaths to innocent bystanders, including children, who are guilty of nothing except being too poor to afford housing in a safer area.

Even in lower-income areas, rising housing costs relative to income are making the poor even poorer.

High rent burdens require families to cut back on other expenses.

"In order to pay their monthly housing costs, low-income households with severe housing cost burdens cut back most heavily on their spending for food, transportation, health care, and retirement savings," according to JCHS. "The lowest-income households spend about $130 less on food each month—a reduction of nearly 40 percent relative to those without housing cost burdens."

In many cases, these households are just one unexpected expense away from missing a rent payment and becoming homeless or having to look for another place they can afford to rent.

They also have to share housing with other people, often with unrelated friends or acquaintances, which means enduring overcrowded living conditions.

Those of us who are well housed may have trouble imagining what it's like to "double up" or triple up in an apartment or house meant for far fewer people. For most people, it is not like moving into the guest room in a friend's suburban ranch house. Doubling up usually involves a poor family living with people who are almost as poor but have a lease. Shared living quarters often don't offer use of a kitchen or easy access to a bathroom. These families lack any shred of security or stability, making it hard for children to stay safe, let alone have success in school.

It's hard for even the most motivated children to study if there is no privacy or quiet, or if they never know for sure when they may have to move again and start attending a new school.

Privacy is nonexistent. It puts enormous strains on everyone involved, especially children. For the host family, there's the risk that the landlord will object to the over-occupancy and kick everyone out of the building. Many landlords overlook overcrowding but neglect maintenance and repairs necessitated by the wear and tear the crowding puts on a building.

Home prices out of reach

The housing affordability problem includes for-sale homes as well as rentals. Home prices bottomed out in 2012, with a national median of $154,000 for existing homes. The median price came roaring back to $212,000 in 2015, and is much higher in many parts of the country.

For example, in the metro area that includes Los Angeles, it was $434,000 in early 2015. In sunny Silicon Valley, it was a whopping

$900,000 at that time, up from $645,000 in 2012.

That means even a modest home is out of reach to many people with moderate incomes, and as interest rates rise, which is widely expected to happen in the coming years, affordability will be even harder to achieve.

Coming up with the required down payment on a loan is also a major obstacle for people of modest means.

A downpayment of 10 or 20 percent of the purchase price is frequently required to buy a home. Coming up with that money is a problem for many blacks and Hispanics. Even a 5 percent downpayment on a $200,000 home is hard to come by for many families.

It's hard to meet that requirement when $11,000 is all you have in the bank. That was the median amount of savings held by black households in 2013.

Among Hispanic houseolds, median wealth was $13,700 in 2013.[27]

Then there is the challenge of qualifying for a mortgage, something that has become significantly harder since the constriction in the availability of credit that followed the foreclosure crisis.

Increasing demand for rentals

The outlook for improved affordability is not encouraging, according to JCHS and other sources of projections on costs and incomes.

"...Absent a dramatic expansion of federal assistance to help defray the costs of renting, or a shift in state and local land use and building regulations to allow expansion of modest, high-density rental developments—affordability problems will remain at staggeringly high levels, if not worsen," according to JCHS.[28]

As the economy started to improve, the number of U.S. households hit 117 million in 2010, up 12 percent from 2000. The number of households will rise again by about 12 million or so from 2010 to 2020, depending on assumptions about immigration, according to JCHS.

New households will drive a surge in demand for housing, but it will fall increasingly on the side of renting rather than owning, thanks to dwindling access to mortgage loans, stalled job prospects, and changes in lifestyles.

For each percentage point decrease in the rate of homeownership, there is a shift of approximately 1.1 million households to the rental market, according to the National Multifamily Housing Council (NMHC) and the National Apartment Association.

They predict that 400,000 or so households will enter the rental market each year through 2020. That does not count those who are homeless or living with friends but would love to have their own apartment if they could afford it.

Incomes for most Americans will not rise nearly as fast as the costs of housing in the coming years. In fact, demographic projections indicate they will rise only marginally, or even stagnate or decline for many people.

Changing demographics will accelerate the shift from ownership to rentals. By 2030, nearly three-quarters of our households will be childless, according to the NMHC. Between 2000 and 2040, fully 86 percent of our household growth will be households without children.

Minority groups with their lower incomes and savings, on average, will also make up a very large percentage of new households, and they will be mostly renters.

It's extremely unlikely that production of new rental housing can come anywhere close to meeting that demand, especially after accounting for the number of older units lost each year to obsolescence and demolition.

New construction typically adds residences at the upper end of the rent distribution. A new apartment with less than 600 square feet in the booming Uptown district of Dallas will set you back almost $1,500 a month. A new one-bedroom in the "hip and trendy" South End of Boston will cost $2,795 per month. If you want to be even hipper and live in the Seaport area, you will pay $3,100 to $3,700 per month for just one bedroom.

These are examples from very popular areas. But even looking at our major urban markets on the whole, you will see median rent levels for a two-bedroom unit increasing dramatically, according to a survey by Trulia. In Miami, the median rent jumped 6.4 percent in one year. In Boston, it went up 5.5 percent.

Less-affluent households have to rely on the stock of older, poorly located, or substandard housing. That supply of housing is declining every year. Of the 34.8 million rentals that existed in 2001, some 1.9 million were demolished by 2011—a loss rate of 5.6 percent, according to JCHS.

Smaller and older rental buildings, which account for high shares of affordable units, are especially vulnerable to loss, JCHS reported.

The losses are certain to continue due to the age of our housing stock. In 2011, the median age of the rental housing buildings in America was 38 years, according to JCHS. "As housing ages, owners must devote an increasing share of rents to maintenance and replacements of aging systems to maintain the structures in adequate condition," JCHS stated.

It's almost impossible to provide new housing affordable to low- and moderate-income people in most parts of our country without the help of a state or federal government subsidy. Even in states that have a free-market orientation that involves light regulation of construction, there are considerable barriers.

If the worst predictions about the impact of climate change come true, and increasing amounts of land are made uninhabitable due to sea level rise, then our ability to produce enough housing will decline further. In such a scenario, the competition will get even more intense for housing in communities that are economically, socially, AND environmentally stable.

CHAPTER TEN

Conspiring Against Affordability

Most Americans don't think much about how their communities came to be the way they are today. We take them for granted, as if they were natural phenomena, like mountains, that just emerged from rock and earth in a predetermined configuration. Many people assume that the cost of housing is the product of some mysterious mathematical inevitability.

The truth is that our communities are carefully engineered. They are the products of policies and political decisions promulgated by citizens and their elected officials. They reflect the economic and social priorities of the voters and taxpayers. The high cost of housing relative to incomes is not an accident; it's the result of years of policy decisions at the state and local levels.

In the 1950s and 1960s, affluent suburban communities made no secret of their position on people of color who sought to live in their communities; they did not want them and would not let them move in.

Today, people in these areas don't talk about the race or nationality of anyone who may wish to move in. But they do regulate housing development and rehabilitation to such an extent as to virtually guarantee that no more than a handful of minority households could ever afford to rent or buy there.

Advocates for affordable housing refer to the many ways that localities push up the cost of housing or block its construction as "exclusionary" land use policies. They say these policies deny minority households the chance to move up economically and socially.

"Good suburban neighborhoods with good schools, where jobs are being created, are like exclusive private clubs. Most poor minorities have no chance of gaining admission thanks in large part to the lack of affordable housing," said Bart Harvey, former CEO of Enterprise

Community Partners, a national financier and developer of affordable housing.

Affluent communities have largely succeeded at blocking affordable housing in significant amounts. They choose to issue building permits for shopping centers but refuse to build housing for the workers in those shops. They import low-wage workers from other towns, which are often located many miles away, where housing is more affordable, forcing workers to commute long distances.

State housing agencies that provide government subsidies to make apartments affordable often take the path of least resistance and approve development sites in lower-income areas of cities or in towns with lower-income populations. These are places where there is already a good supply of low-cost housing.

This perpetuates a situation in which the limited supply of affordable housing that exists is usually located in the worst parts of the poorest communities, whether they be inner cities or inner suburbs – places where schools do not perform well, crime is high, and jobs are hard to come by or get to.

It's not hard to figure out that by preventing construction of affordable housing and keeping average rents and prices high, exclusionary policies have a disproportionate impact on minorities.

In 2012, the median U.S. income was $57,009 for white households, $33,321 for black households, and $39,005 for Hispanic households. In many metro areas, the income disparity is even greater.

The median income of minority households fell 9 percent from 2010 to 2013, compared with a decrease of 1 percent for white households.

If a black family can afford to pay for a home or apartment, landlords and sellers can no longer legally refuse to rent or sell to them. But there is little the government can do to charge a local government with discrimination if it just happens that the locality contains no housing affordable to most black households.

This form of de facto, or invisible, segregation can be found all over America, from the backyard of a former U. S. president to the affluent towns of Silicon Valley. It is built into the American system of land-use planning and real estate development, and it's not likely to change soon. On the contrary, the rapid escalation of housing costs coupled with the stagnation in the household income and savings of black households means that it will get far worse before it gets better.

"An army of regulators at every level of government is choking off the supply of affordable housing," said Jack Kemp in 1992. Kemp was a member of Congress and served as secretary of HUD.

He was referring to the fact that local governments add costs to housing by virtue of their control over how land may be used and how buildings should be designed and constructed, as well as their fees to provide basic utilities like water and sewage treatment.[29]

Stacking the deck on housing

Conservative politicians love to condemn government housing subsidies as if they are misguided interventions in a free market that is otherwise pure and fair. They overlook the many ways in which the supposedly unbiased private market is stacked against less-affluent people:

- Homeownership is heavily subsidized by state and federal governments, far more than rental housing. These subsidies keep growing while assistance for lower-income people keeps getting cut.

- In many states, systems of taxation put a higher financial burden on new residents who move into a town vs. those who have lived there for a long time, and encourage retail development over housing development.

- Many local governments welcome construction of single-family homes on large lots, but impose major obstacles to construction of multifamily housing, which includes most low-cost rentals.

- Certain elements of the mortgage lending industry have repeatedly taken economic advantage of less-sophisticated households with lower incomes, and government efforts at consumer protection have not been very effective.

Over the years, housing development has become one of the most heavily regulated industries in America. The web of local, state, and federal regulation has grown steadily.

The list of things that drive up housing costs and prevent development of affordable housing goes on and on. It includes:
- The way localities finance infrastructure like sewer and water systems

- Environmental review requirements and remediation of environmental impacts
- Excessive design and construction requirements
- Green building mandates
- Limits on the number of housing units that can be built on each acre of land
- Restrictions on the use of manufactured housing.
- Rigid opposition to multistory, multifamily housing, the type of construction that's most useful in producing affordable rents

All these practices favor the people who already live in a community and work against anyone else moving in, especially those with less income and less wealth.

The most fundamental problem is that federal, state, and local governments keep adding costs to housing, with no constraints and very little discussion about the impact it has on our housing shortage.

How we keep costs high

The process of getting a proposed housing development from the conceptual stage into actual construction is referred to as the "entitlement" process. The developer of the housing, working with architects and other professionals, must go through a long process that includes reviews by a dozen or more agencies and departments. Some of the steps include review of project plans against zoning codes, design standards, environmental requirements, and many other regulations.

The process theoretically ends with the issuance of a building permit, but there is rarely any assurance that a permit will ultimately be issued or how many units it will allow to be built.

Obtaining a building permit for a housing development of any size can easily take years and cost upwards of $500,000 to $1,000,000.

That's only counting the direct costs of working through the entitlement process. During the time that takes, construction costs may rise significantly. Interest expenses on loans continue to add up month after month. The cost of keeping an option on the building site adds up and may increase.

The range of regulations, policies, fees, and processes that affect housing costs would fill an entire book – make that several books. They come from every level of government, from special taxing districts to cities, then regional agencies, state governments, and, finally, federal agencies, most notably the Environmental Protection Agency.

Regulations cover land use, density, the size of lots for detached homes, design standards, building materials, construction methods, and much more. Everything any agency has to review or process comes with a price tag attached, both in fees and in time taken for processing.

Environmental mandates have expanded steadily since the 1970s, most recently to include energy efficiency and reduction of greenhouse gas emissions, recycling of building materials, and other things. California has some of the highest housing costs in the nation partly because it has the most stringent environmental review requirements. New York State is a close second.

Land, costly land

The cost of land accounts for 10 percent to 30 percent of the cost of housing. In communities and neighborhoods that are the most desirable places to live, the costs are on the high end of that range.

Local governments have traditionally controlled policies on how land is used in America through their zoning codes, and increasingly, by ad hoc political decisions on each individual project that is proposed. That gives them control over what can be built and at what cost new housing construction can be delivered to consumers.

Typically, low-rise apartment or townhouses are built at 15 to 35 units per acre, while mid-rise garden apartments are constructed at 40 to 100 units per acre. The higher the number of units that can be built per acre of land, the lower the cost per unit of housing.

Higher density also makes efficient use of infrastructure, like streets and sewers.

The problem is that higher density is not politically acceptable in most areas outside the central cities of our country. In the suburbs, it's generally met with strenuous opposition.

In many affluent areas, any proposal to allow construction of buildings of three or more stories engenders angry political opposition.

Zoning restrictions have been used in many suburban areas to create communities dominated by single-family homes and to exclude rental housing. A standard policy is to require as much as a half-acre of land for each housing unit that can be built.

One of the most detailed analyses of the problem of exclusionary zoning policies was compiled by the United States Commission on Civil Rights in a report titled, *Equal Opportunity in Suburbia*. It was based on hearings in three cities that included testimony from over 150 witnesses, ranging from welfare mothers to cabinet secretaries. Published in 1974, the report summarized the situation very clearly:

> While many local governments would object to any diminution of their control over the use of land, the present system of zoning controls is in clear need of modification. Suburban zoning has had the effect both of displacing and of excluding low-income and minority families, and its use toward this end has often been intentional.[31]

In 1992, a commission appointed by President Bush came to a very similar conclusion. Since then, the problem of local restrictions on density has not improved and in many areas, has gotten worse.

As one member of the commission wrote, prohibitions against housing developments with moderate or high density are "one of the most widespread and serious regulatory barriers to housing affordability."[30]

Very little changed since the 1974 report was issued. Ditto for the 1992 commission report. The courts have consistently held that local governments can generally do as they please in determining their land use policies, and the federal government has done nothing to change that.

Reliance on property taxes

Most local governments rely heavily on property taxes to pay for government operations and schools. That's a key reason they tend to favor policies that push housing prices up and keep them on an upward trajectory.

Local governments assume that development of low-cost rentals will have a negative impact on property values. This assumption is not supported by empirical evidence. In fact, studies have shown that recently constructed, high quality affordable housing generally has no negative effect on property values, and sometimes has a positive one.

In some areas, property tax systems also drive up the cost of owning a home quite a bit. In California, Proposition 13 was passed by the voters in 1978 to impose limits on how much property taxes can be raised each year.

That means that as long as a family stays in one house, the increases in their taxes are tightly limited. Thus, a city's financial needs must be met by raising taxes primarily when homes are sold. This means that families who wish to buy homes face higher and higher taxes.

This system limits the tax revenue flowing to local governments, causing them to scramble for other ways to cover the cost of basic infrastructure, like streets and sewers. These costs often have a powerful inflationary impact on the cost of rental housing development.

Sales taxes are also an important source of local revenue. As a result, in many localities, housing is the least lucrative use of land for a local government since it doesn't generate sales taxes.

Buildings and designs

Homeowners who have dealt with their local zoning or building departments to get approval for an addition to their home know that it can be a slow and expensive process. But it's a tiny taste of what happens to developers of larger properties that add to our housing stock.

There has been progress in standardizing basic building codes in America. However, that trend has been offset by the increasing breadth of what local officials choose to regulate, and what state legislators direct them to regulate. Design and construction requirements get more onerous and more expensive to meet year after year.

They are particularly problematic when they are assessed on the number of housing units being built rather than on the value of the property.

As codes have become more comprehensive, adding provisions on everything from seismic safety and water conservation to handling of construction waste, the incremental addition to construction costs has increased.

Building codes in most places discourage rehabilitation of older housing, and that means owners are more likely to let their properties decay to the point of obsolescence and demolition, rather than restore them to viable use as lower-cost housing.

Infill development on empty lots in existing built-up areas is a great way to provide housing that taps into existing infrastructure and transportation systems while reducing demands on open space.

But building and land use laws often make infill impossible to do, since projects are often small and can't carry all the extra costs. One example is local requirements for a large number of parking spaces per unit of housing, which adds substantial costs.

The task of constructing and maintaining infrastructure like sewer and water systems is another major contributor to the increased costs of housing.

In the past, cities created these facilities and then levied taxes on all the properties in town to pay for them. But when taxpayers rebelled against increases in their taxes, cities could no longer easily finance expansion or maintenance of these facilities. In response, they shifted the burden of paying for them to new real estate developments.

The problem is that, instead of paying just for the share of infrastructure costs related to a proposed development, builders are often required to pay for improvements that serve entire neighborhoods or even entire towns.

These costs take the form of either impact fees, which go to the public agencies that build and operate the facilities, or requirements that developers build the infrastructure at their sole expense.

No help from Washington

What's the federal government doing to reduce the inflationary impact of state and local government policies? Nothing. On the contrary, Congress and the federal courts have generally added to the regulatory burden rather than reducing it.

There was some hope for progress when President Bush appointed his Advisory Commission on Regulatory Barriers to Affordable Housing. The panel produced a detailed report with dozens of recommendations. It said that excessive fees and regulations were increasing housing costs by around 25 percent. One panel member said the incremental increase in costs was 50 percent, and possibly even more.

The commission's recommendations for change were aggressively promoted. The chief advocate was Jack Kemp, an articulate, former congressman and football star from Buffalo, N.Y. He was Secretary of the Department of Housing and Urban Development at the time, and he believed strongly in the substance of the report.

But despite his best efforts to use his fame and charisma to promote the cause of deregulation, Kemp could not convince Congress to do anything about it. Since Kemp's day, no politician of any prominence has shown an interest in fighting for change in local policies.

Meanwhile, the problems cited by the commission have gotten worse.

Twenty-one years after the Bush commission report, the same concerns were echoed by the Bipartisan Policy Center's Housing Commission. It said that excessive regulation and fees were preventing development of "rental housing that could help meet the needs of moderate-income households and allow older developments to filter down to rent levels affordable to low-income households."[32]

• • •

All the regulations and fees the localities impose on affordable housing have legitimate or well-established rationales. But these myriad regulations and fees are piled on one after the other with no cost-benefit analysis. Very few local agencies stop to analyze how they will affect housing affordability.

In Washington, no one totals up how much new regulations and increased fees add to the cost of housing each year. No one looks at the impact on housing affordability even for federally-assisted developments. Local agencies have carte blanche in deciding how many financial hurdles to put in the way of housing development, reducing overall production and driving up the cost of however many housing units do get constructed.

Since the 1950s, study after study has found that a key step to ending the separation of Americans into two societies that are separate and unequal is to make sure that affordable housing is created outside areas where poverty is already concentrated.

Affluent, mostly white, and mostly suburban communities must allow affordable housing to be developed, and federal programs must be oriented toward providing housing in those places.

The Kerner Commission said it particularly clearly:

> Enactment of a fair housing law will eliminate the most obvious barrier limiting the areas in which nonwhites can live, but it will not deal with an equally impenetrable barrier: the unavailability of low and moderate income housing in nonghetto areas.

The commission called for six million new affordable housing units to be made available over the five years after it reported, but said most of them needed to be located outside of the central cities. Despite this and many other calls for dispersion of affordable housing, it has not happened to any extent. The invisible wall preventing housing development in suburban areas has not come down. It's gotten higher and stronger, and the federal government has done very little to change that.

CHAPTER ELEVEN

The Politics of Housing

Public opinion polls show that most Americans think affordable housing is important to the success of communities, not to mention their own children's futures. But when it comes to a specific development planned in their own community, affordable housing is about as welcome as a nuclear waste dump. Nobody wants it to be built near them.

The people who dislike affordable housing are often in firm control of land use, zoning, and building permit processes for privately developed housing. They can use those powers to ensure that if any new market-rate housing is built, it will be too costly for low- and moderate-income people. This is as routine as collecting taxes.

Grassroots opposition to housing emerges like an army waiting in ambush when a housing project with state or federal government subsidies is proposed.

The routine of driving up development costs may not stop a subsidized project from being built. The government has deep pockets and will cover the higher costs, so more aggressive political tactics are often employed.

This kind of opposition to affordable rental housing development has been growing more powerful and more pervasive for years, even as the need for that housing has increased dramatically.

It's often referred to as NIMBY, which stands for "not in my backyard," which is the typical response given when a city proposes to allow subsidized housing development.

The Advisory Commission on Regulatory Barriers to Affordable Housing said that neutralizing the power of NIMBY to block housing development was critical to meeting our nation's affordable housing needs.

NIMBY sentiment [is] frequently widespread and deeply ingrained. [It] is so powerful because it is easily translatable into government action, given the existing system for regulating land use and development. Current residents and organized neighborhood groups can exert great influence over local electoral and land-development processes, to the exclusion of nonresidents, prospective residents, or, for that matter, all outsiders. Restrictions on affordable housing [development] are the result.

With the winds of opposition to affordable housing howling, cities often use their regulatory and fee-charging powers to prevent construction of affordable housing. A favorite tactic is to delay the issuance of a building permit for so long that the developer or the state housing agency financing the project simply gives up and chooses a location where the resistance is less powerful. That ususally means a lower-income town where there already is affordable housing. Thus, once again, the concentration of poverty is perpetuated.

No project is safe from the power of NIMBY. Even developers who want to put up homes for veterans of our armed services can't escape. One nonprofit group tried to build such a facility right next door to the Department of Veteran's Affairs hospital in Omaha, Neb. The affluent owners of homes in the neighborhood obtained a court order stating that it could not be built. The sponsor could not afford the lengthy legal process that would have been required to overturn that court order.

• • •

Most cities and counties have some sort of long-range plan for how they will manage land use as they grow. But political opposition to affordable housing has become increasingly strident, and less and less connected to the long-range planning process. Time after time, local residents rise up in opposition to specific development proposals whether they conform to adopted plans or not.

If a mayor or city council suggests that it might allow subsidized housing to be built within its borders, anti-housing activists turn out in force at any public hearing. They often vote out of office any official who appears too "soft" on the anti-housing platform.

In Marin County, Calif., for example, a county supervisor consistently fought all proposals for affordable housing development. After a few years in office, she softened her position. She said it made sense to redevelop an empty shopping center to provide low-cost apartments for people working in that area in retail and other low paying jobs. She was promptly voted out of office because she had shown a tolerance of housing development.

Today's opposition to affordable housing is almost always explained in terms of the complex nature of our built environment today. NIMBY factions often say their opposition has to do with building size, the impact on traffic, design, environmental impacts, and other physical ramifications of construction, and not the race or income of the people who would live in the housing.

But while today's opponents of affordable housing may not consciously intend to perpetuate segregated communities in the same way the avowed segregationists of the '50s and '60s did, their positions very often lead to similar outcomes.

• • •

To the extent that subsidized housing is allowed in a community, it would be affordable to many people of color, and the owners, having received government subsidies, would generally be required to advertise the availability of that housing on a nondiscriminatory basis.

Sometimes, the racial animosity is only just inches below the surface of the discussion about a project. In the New Orleans metropolitan area, shortly after Hurricane Katrina hit, many people worked very hard to make up for the loss of housing. Some people did not share in the general desire to help.

In one community just across the Mississippi River from the ravaged Lower Ninth Ward, a nonprofit, faith-based group proposed to build low-rent apartments for elders, many of whom had lost their homes in the city after the hurricane.

The local reception to the project was extremely hostile. There was a standing room only meeting at a senior citizens center. The crowd was all white except for one person of color, and would not even give the developer a chance to describe the proposed project.

The woman who spoke for the nonprofit sponsor recalled what happened after the leading politician opposed to the project had spoken and she got up to speak:

He had those people in a frenzy and I could not make my presentation. I was not allowed to complete a sentence without being booed
or shouted down.

The project was never built, and at last report, there was still no
affordable rental housing available in the community.

• • •

Some state legislators and some courts have recognized that the
Fair Housing Act was insufficient to keep the doors open to residential mobility among poor minorities. Massachusetts, New Jersey, and
several other states have enacted laws that empower developers or
state authorities to override local zoning to ensure that affordable
housing is provided.

At the federal level, HUD uses its grant money to influence local
decisions on affordable housing across the country. It requires, as a
condition of its grants, recipients to proactively work to provide housing for people of all races in their community. HUD calls it "affirmatively furthering fair housing."

Many metropolitan areas have undertaken planning efforts that
call for increasing overall density and dedicated efforts to provide
more affordable housing, including measures to convince individual
local governments to go along with those plans. The efforts are often
described as "sustainable communities" planning.

But all of these efforts face very powerful political resistance. Local politicians know they can win political points by lashing out at
"big government" for interfering in local decisions about land use.

They play on fear and bias to gain votes, and use affordable housing as their straw man. Very few local officials are willing to stick
their political necks out by actively supporting affordable housing.

Even generalized planning for higher density housing districts
meets strong opposition from people who describe it as an attack on
the American "way of life." They have referred to higher density as
"stack and pack," accused the federal government of waging a "war
on suburbia" and even suggested that President Obama wanted to
start a "race war."

One of the more moderate organizations fighting planning for
higher density is the Pacific Legal Foundation in California. Its views
were reflected in a statement by Damien Schiff, the organization's
principal attorney:

In this planner's dream environment, everyone would complacently agree to a regimented lifestyle, living in multi-family housing, and walking, bike-riding, or taking public transit to work. The drafting agencies have come up with an ambitious strategy to micro-manage people's lifestyle choices.

Taken together, anti-housing attitudes and onerous regulatory policies have a snowball effect. The more difficult anti-housing groups make it to build, the fewer organizations try to undertake the long, expensive process of development, with all the risk it entails. Many small nonprofit housing developers, including faith-based groups, have simply gone out of business. Small, for-profit builders are not doing much better.

Elected officials are often too intimidated by these anti-housing activists to do the hard work required to win acceptance of higher density and inclusionary policies that reduce costs and encourage affordable housing.

By reducing affordable housing availability, NIMBYs erect an invisible barrier. It says to every young person from a lower-income or minority family that, no matter how personally virtuous they are, they cannot live in places with decent employment and educational opportunities—unless, of course, they happen to get rich enough to buy a single-family home.

The Politics of Fear

CHAPTER TWELVE

The Last Gasp of Liberalism

The day after Martin Luther King, Jr. died, President Johnson wrote to the speaker of the House of Representatives to ask for an immediate vote on legislation outlawing discrimination in housing. He had been pushing for such a bill for several years without success. This time, he was determined to win.

"Last night, America was shocked by a senseless act of violence. A man who devoted his life to the nonviolent achievement of rights that most Americans take for granted was killed by an assassin's bullet," Johnson wrote.[1]

"When the nation so urgently needs the healing balm of unity, a brutal wound on our conscience forces upon us all this question: 'What more can I do to achieve brotherhood and equality among all Americans?'"

King's funeral took place in Atlanta on April 9, 1968. On the next day, the House voted by a wide margin to adopt the Civil Rights Act of 1968. It had already cleared the Senate and was quickly signed into law. Title VIII of the law is commonly known as the Fair Housing Act. It prohibits discrimination in the sale, rental, and financing of housing based on race, religion, or national origin.

Meanwhile, in southeast Washington, construction was nearing completion on the building that would house the agency in charge of enforcing the new fair housing law and running housing and urban programs. The Department of Housing and Urban Development (HUD) had been working out of temporary quarters since it started doing business in 1966. Two years later, it was ready to enter the national stage with a flourish.

On the morning of Aug. 1, 1968, Johnson went to the plaza of the sparkling new HUD building to sign a new law making comprehensive improvements and additions to housing and urban programs. The Housing and Urban Development Act of 1968 created a wide array of new government programs intended to eliminate slum conditions in America's cities.

The law reaffirmed the "national housing goal," which says that every American should have "a decent home and a suitable living environment." To help achieve that, the law committed the U.S. to produce 2.6 million units of new and rehabilitated housing each year, including 600,000 units for low-income families. The law created a comprehensive set of programs designed to meet that goal, help people rent existing housing, revitalize urban communities, and more.[2]

Robert Weaver, the first secretary of HUD, was celebrated as the primary author of this landmark new law. Johnson was so proud of the new law and the new building that he waxed poetic about what it all represented for American cities and race relations.

"We know that a home is more than a shelter," he said. "Through dozens of other programs we are trying to work to improve the quality of man's life and to better humanity. But the center of our effort is here--the center of man's life--the place we all call our home," he said.[3]

"I believe that history will mark this first day of August 1968, as the day and the time and the moment when farsighted people turned the clock ahead, setting the hands of progress to the tempo of man's racing needs," Johnson concluded.[4]

Johnson firmly believed that having good housing was a key step to help people advance their situation in life.

He knew that jobs and education were important, but he and Weaver believed that good–quality, affordable housing that was not concentrated in the ghettos was critical to begin reversing the corrosive effect of concentrated poverty and separation from white society.

Goodbye to old ways

The new agency and the new housing and community development programs enacted between 1965 and 1968 would help change the U.S. government from an ally of segregationists to a powerful force for integration. They would also move us toward the rehabilitation and revitalization of urban areas and away from the previous focus on demolition and redevelopment for mega projects.

It was a moment of triumph for Johnson and the people HUD was created to serve. But the celebration was not destined to last long. A political sea change was roiling that summer as the country prepared to elect a new president.

As the 1968 election neared, the debate over the cities and race was reduced to this two-part question: Did the federal government need to do a great deal more to help blacks advance their lives, obtain decent housing, and move out of the segregated ghettos into better areas, including the suburbs? Or had the riots proved that the liberal social programs of the Kennedy-Johnson era had failed miserably and that there was no point throwing good money after bad?

Representing the first position was Hubert Humphrey, Johnson's vice president, and the obvious choice to be the Democratic nominee for president.

Humphrey's campaign managers were Fred Harris, a young U.S. senator who served on the Kerner Commission, and Walter Mondale, a senator who was a key advocate for fair housing legislation, both then and in subsequent years.

Suburbia rules

Representing the other side of the argument were Richard Nixon and Ronald Reagan, the conservatives contending for the Republican nomination. Alabama Governor George Wallace ran as an independent.

Nixon realized that suburban voters outnumbered those living in central cities for the first time, and he played to them for his victory. He was convinced that this mostly white voting bloc wanted to know how the government would protect them from the ghettos' residents – not about how to improve the ghettos.[5]

When the Kerner Commission talked about two societies, it meant that they should be merged into one. But Nixon knew that white voters took away something quite different from that widely quoted statement. If there were two societies, white people wanted to be sure their society remained out on top and retained its privileges.[6]

Nixon cast himself as the ally of whites who were resentful of government assistance going to blacks and fearful after seeing the violence of the riots:

We have been warned that we face the prospect of a war in the making in our own society. We have seen the gathering hate. We have heard the threats to burn, bomb and destroy. In Watts, Harlem and Detroit and Newark, we have had a foretaste of what the organizers of insurrection are planning for the summer. We must take the warnings to heart and be prepared to meet force with force if necessary.[7]

Nixon won the New Hampshire Republican primary by a huge margin.

When the Republican convention convened in August in Miami Beach, the course of the nation was foretold in a speech by the governor of California at the time, an actor-turned-politician named Ronald Reagan.

"We must reject the idea that every time the law is broken, society is guilty rather than the lawbreaker," Reagan said. "It is time to move against these destructive dissidents; it is time to say, 'Obey the rules or get out.'"[8]

On Nov. 5, 1968, Nixon was elected president. He took office in January 1969.

Four years after Johnson's call for us to strive to be a better nation, Nixon set a far different tone in his inaugural address, one that reflected drastically lowered expectations.

"In these difficult years, America has suffered from a fever of words; from inflated rhetoric that promises more than it can deliver, from angry rhetoric that fans discontents into hatreds, from bombastic rhetoric that postures instead of persuading." He said, "We are approaching the limits of what government alone can do."[9]

• • •

As 1969 began, Lyndon Johnson's vision of America as a "great society" was as battered as the boarded-up buildings of riot-torn 14th Street in Washington, D.C.

Years later, Ronald Reagan would say that Johnson declared war on poverty and "poverty won." It would have been more accurate to say that the opponents of aggressive action to address racial inequality and urban decay had won.

The steady progress toward constructive political dialog about race relations, the poor, and the cities where they lived was over. The gradual awakening of whites to the need for civil rights and more opportunities for blacks had hit a brick wall of fear and distrust.

Nixon moved into the White House under the new paradigm that Americans wanted more law and order and less spending on social programs.

The shift that took place under Nixon and later under Reagan represented a smashing victory for those who had opposed Johnson's social justice agenda all along. They had been gaining power for some time, and while King's death brought a temporary truce, it did not change the deep-seated distrust many felt for social programs and racial integration.

The Kerner report came out in February of 1968, just as the U.S. Senate was working out a compromise on the language of the Fair Housing Act. The confluence of events seemed like the end of the world to conservatives in general and to white southerners in particular.

"Passage of this open-housing legislation...will prove to be a grave mistake, and one of the gravest that the Senate has ever made," said Sen. John Stennis (D-Miss.). "I will have no part of it and I am confident it will be repudiated, eventually, by the people in overwhelming numbers at the polls."

Stennis railed against the idea that, under the law, HUD would be given the power to tell people what to do with their private property, that is, to tell them they could not refuse to rent or sell to a person solely because of their race. "This bill strikes down one of the basic rights of all American citizens – the right of ownership over his private property," Stennis said.

Another Southerner articulated the fear on the part of whites that African Americans would use the Kerner Commission report to foment violent revolution. Sen. Allen J. Ellender, (D-La.) said:

Racial demagogues and agitators will set out across the length and breadth of the nation. At every stop, they will be able to point to the commission's report and recommendations, an official government document. They will be able to say to their audiences and followers: 'Here is what you have been deprived of. Here is what this country has denied you. Your plight and troubles are not your fault, but the fault of American society. If the country will not give you what you deserve, when are you going to stand up and take it for yourself?'

Ellender was not alone in expressing fear about increased black militancy. Even Washington liberals were stunned by how blunt the commission's report had been, mincing no words in blaming "white racism" for the problems of the black ghettos. It detailed the ways in which white society had marginalized ghetto residents, including police brutality and denial of political power.

President Johnson had appointed the panel but did not lobby Congress to adopt its recommendations. He had expected the panel to be circumspect and cautious. He had expected it to understand that the budget constraints caused by spending on the Vietnam War would not allow massive new spending to help cities and blacks.

He also believed that incremental progress on civil rights was the best that could be achieved, and that blaming white people in general for the problems of blacks would not help.

Johnson was so troubled by the report that he refused to even sign "thank you" letters to the men who had served on the panel, according to *At Canaan's Edge*, by Taylor Branch.

Republicans and Southern Democrats condemned the report for justifying violence and dismissed its conclusions out of hand. They argued that the riots were proof that liberal social policies intended to help the poor had actually made things worse – and not, as liberals and Kerner had stated, that much more needed to be done.

Reversing course

The massive commitment of government funds that Kerner recommended was not made. On the contrary, as soon as Johnson was out of office, his opponents began a gradual and very tenacious effort to roll back the programs that had already been put in place.

The 1968 housing act had set an ambitious goal for production of affordable housing, but actual annual production approached those levels only a few times, and before long, the goal was forgotten (even though it stayed on the books as official U.S. policy).

Likewise, although the Fair Housing Act had been passed, there was concerted opposition to vigorous enforcement of its provisions.

Congress had authorized the creation of HUD, but the legislative body was always divided on whether it was such a good idea.

In 1965, only 10 out of 139 Republicans in the House voted for H.R. 6927, the bill that created HUD as a cabinet-level department. That's just 7 percent of the Republicans in the House; and for the most part, the Republicans who followed them have continued to be skeptical of HUD, if not against it. Southern Democrats weren't big fans of the agency either.

The agency has fared much better in Democratic-controlled Congresses, but the ongoing division of opinion on HUD that existed in 1965 has never gone away.

The attacks on proposed spending for HUD programs began almost immediately after its creation. One of the first acts of Congress on behalf of the new agency was to give it only 50 percent of the funding the Johnson administration requested for the ambitious Model Cities program. It was a sign of things to come.

Limits of the law

Meanwhile, the limits of what had been achieved to enforce the fair housing law also became apparent. The 1968 fair housing law was weak to begin with, since it gave HUD no power to force any landlord or home seller to change discriminatory behavior.

When someone brought a complaint to HUD, all the staff could do was to arrange voluntary discussions with the landlord or property owner involved. It had no power to impose a settlement or punish anyone who broke the law.

But even that weak law was not something Congress really wanted HUD to enforce.

In the budget request process for 1969, Weaver asked for $11 million in funding to hire 850 people to start the process of handling fair housing complaints on a nationwide basis. Congress appropriated only $2 million, less than 20 percent of what Weaver believed was needed. Many of the people who had waited and hoped for a federal effort to ensure fair housing would have to wait a lot longer.[10]

Real estate agents and property owners could continue to discriminate against people of color with little concern that their victims would be able to obtain relief from HUD.

Years later, in 1977, Democrats proposed measures to give HUD actual enforcement powers for dealing with fair housing violations. It was not until 1988, 20 years after the original law was passed, that Congress finally enacted this amendment. It also expanded the coverage of the law to include the handicapped and families with children.

As part of that debate, HUD studied the extent of racial discrimination in housing and estimated that 2 million people, primarily blacks, experienced housing discrimination every year.

CHAPTER THIRTEEN

An Easy Target for Attack

Fifty years after HUD was created, it's time to ask why so many politicians opposed the existence of a housing and urban agency, and why so many have tried to cripple or kill off its programs over the last half century. Is HUD really as ineffective as its critics say? Or could it be that HUD has been TOO effective in helping people who some in Congress don't see as deserving?

To unravel that mystery, first consider the timing of HUD's birth. It was legally authorized in 1965 and began operations in 1966 – well after the cities had decayed to a substantial extent.

For most of the period of "The Great Migration" (the influx of southern African Americans into northern cities), little was done to help cities provide housing and public facilities for the newcomers. HUD should have been created right after World War II to have successfully headed off or slowed urban decay.

To put it in context, consider this: We did not wait until the Dust Bowl ravaged American farming in the 1930s before we created the Agriculture Department. Congress authorized that agency in 1889. Its programs to develop rural areas and support farm families and workers with housing had been operating for 75 years before HUD was created.

Asking HUD to move from getting organized as a federal cabinet department to showing major progress on complex urban problems in a couple of years seems absurd, but that's just what Congress did. Expectations were extremely high, and the judgment of the agency for its initial performance was very harsh.

One could say that HUD was born under a bad sign. It started doing business during a period of violent urban unrest and intense political arguments about race, housing, and the cities. The agency had to deal with much more than just the physical aspects of cities and metropolitan areas. It was caught up from the start in the enormous challenge of sorting out race relations in America.

Politically, HUD has always been seen as the agency that serves African Americans who live in the cities, a generally Democratic constituency. This never sat well with some factions in Congress. The issue of race was made even more prominent when Johnson chose a black man to run the agency. It was the first time a black man had served at the level of a cabinet secretary in the U.S. government.

No one could have been as prepared for that job as Robert Weaver.

Housing before HUD

The biggest federal housing programs before HUD was created were the insurance of mortgages on homes and apartment buildings through the Federal Housing Administration, which started in 1934, and the development of public housing, which began in 1937. Federal investment in urban redevelopment began in 1949.

All of these programs were subject to heavy criticism that they contributed to the concentration of poverty in the inner cities and the expansion of suburban communities that were almost always for whites only.

It was only after HUD was created and took over these programs that the federal government took a more constructive role in revitalizing cities and creating housing opportunities for people of all races.

He had been involved in federal housing programs for decades, and was the director of the Housing and Home Finance Agency, which was absorbed into HUD.

He knew how to play the political game. But at HUD, he was between a rock and a hard place. He was under enormous pressure from liberals to work miracles with a limited budget. Republicans and Southern Democrats felt HUD had too much power and that its programs were too costly, and worked to limit its power and funding.

HUD has faced relentless attacks from Congress since Weaver's day. During the federal budgeting process, Republican members of

Congress routinely try to cut appropriations for the agency's programs or eliminate them altogether. Sometimes Democratic presidents go along with the cuts, depending on which way the political
winds are blowing.

When the Fair Housing Act was passed in 1968, HUD was handed
responsibility for enforcing the law. That was another strike against
the agency in the eyes of many members of Congress.

If all those political headwinds were not difficult enough, HUD
had to operate as a government agency as well as a business – a nearly impossible task. It had to comply with congressionally mandated
red tape and yet also deal with the economic challenges of financing
and owning real estate, a challenging business full of risks and reek-
ing of private-sector opportunism.

It had to try to enforce its policies and rules on some of the most
self-interested people in America – big city mayors, real estate owners, brokers, and bankers. The political and profit motives at work
have always made it hard for HUD bureaucrats to keep everyone
honest.

On top of that, HUD had to deal with the political pressures applied by members of Congress to help their local supporters with
their real estate projects. In one rather infamous case, a certain
member of Congress was talking publicly about terminating HUD's
existence while working privately to get the agency to help one of his
supporters. He wasn't the only one to attack the agency while trying
to get maximum benefit out of it for his allies.

Opening doors to suburbia

When the Kerner Commission made its report on the problem of
the cities, it was quite clear about the policy choices the federal government needed to make. We could try to improve conditions in the
ghettos by encouraging job creation, bringing in social services, and
rehabilitating older housing. Or we could provide housing subsidies
in such a way as to encourage ghetto residents to leave those places and relocate to areas with better housing, better schools, safer
streets and such.

The commission said the first approach was good but not sufficient. It said the federal government needed to build 6 million units
of affordable housing over five years – or about 1.2 million units a
year – and that this housing had to be located throughout each of our

metropolitan areas, including the white suburbs.

It warned that continuation of the previous practice of building poor–quality, high-rise public housing in the inner cities would only further concentrate poverty and exacerbate the social problems and dysfunction that already existed.

The only problem was that the suburbs did not want anything to do with this plan. Convincing them otherwise would fall to HUD.

The main goal of the Fair Housing Act of 1968 was to stop individual instances of housing discrimination. But it also contained language that empowered HUD to use its grant programs to "affirmatively further" fair housing. That meant HUD could use the billions of dollars in government grants it disbursed as leverage to get local governments to remove regulatory obstacles to creation of affordable housing.

One man took that opportunity very seriously and was willing to stand up to a president to try to use that power to change things. His name was George Romney, the father of the recent presidential candidate Mitt Romney. The senior Romney was governor of Michigan during the riots of 1967 and 1968, and became secretary of HUD under President Nixon in January 1969.

Visiting the ghettos

Romney had run a brief campaign of his own for the Republican presidential nomination. As part of that campaign, he visited ghetto areas in 17 American cities to see conditions there firsthand.

As governor, Romney strongly supported civil rights and worked to help lower-income people gain access to housing outside the central cities. He fought for passage of a state law to encourage suburban communities to allow low-rent housing construction, saying it was the only way to relieve the terrible conditions in the ghettos of places like Detroit.

When Romney became the third secretary of HUD, he was in exactly the right place at the right time to use federal power to break down the obstacles to affordable housing in suburbia.

He moved quickly and quietly to institute an "open communities" program based on a simple premise: If a town wanted to receive grants from HUD for sewers or other projects, it had to show that it was not obstructing development of affordable housing. If a locality did not allow construction of affordable housing and make it available to blacks and Hispanics, that town's grant money would be withheld.

One of Romney's first attempts to implement the policy was in his own state. HUD was about to award $3 million in urban renewal funding for the town of Warren, Mich., which was 99 percent white. Romney ordered the money to be withheld until and unless the city allowed construction of affordable housing.

It was a gutsy move considering the history of the place. It had only been six years since an incident that showed how the local people felt about letting black families live in their town. An angry mob of white people had surrounded the home of a black family that had managed to buy a home there. When the local cops wouldn't disperse the crowd, Romney had to send the Michigan State Police to do it.[11]

Nixon had never endorsed what Romney was doing. When he found out, he ordered Romney to stop using federal grants to pressure suburban governments to accept affordable housing. Nixon said there would be no requirements imposed on any suburban government to change their "exclusionary" policies in order to get federal money.

Romney refused to back down, according to one account. He stayed at HUD and kept pushing local governments to stop obstructing affordable housing. Finally, after continued pressure from Nixon, Romney gave up the fight and resigned in November 1972.

Appeasing suburban voters

Nixon understood the politics of affordable housing and suburban governments well enough. Suburban communities that kept out affordable housing were adamant about their right to continue doing so. They showed their willingness to fight any federal attempt to convince them otherwise in the 1960s and they continue to do so today.

The failure of the Fair Housing Act to bring systemic change in where low-cost housing could be built was predictable. The law was passed largely out of respect for Martin Luther King, Jr., and because it included a provision allowing federal prosecution of anyone who traveled across state lines to "incite" a riot. It was not because a solid majority of members of Congress fully supported fair housing.

Over time, the part of the law relating to individual cases of blatant discrimination against individuals has become an accepted part of U.S. law. But the idea that the federal government should have any

leverage over local land use decisions regarding affordable housing
has never been widely accepted.

If Romney had been president instead of Nixon, things could
have turned out much differently. Romney hoped to ask Congress
to give HUD the power to legally override local zoning codes that
blocked affordable housing development. It would have been a much
more direct approach than withholding grant money.

But Nixon was the president, and he made certain that suburban
communities were not made "open." The consequences have been
felt not just by minority households, but by all the taxpayers of affected areas, according to an essay by Gregory D. Squires, professor
of sociology and public policy at George Washingon University.

> The persistence of barrios and ghettos in the nation's metropolitan
> areas...undercuts the economic growth, political stability and so-
> cial development of entire regions. Cities with large poor popula-
> tions and high levels of concentrated poverty pay more for a range
> of public services, including education, police, health care, fire pro-
> tection, which increases taxes and reduces their ability to attract
> middle-class families.[12]

After he crushed Romney's vision of open communities, Nixon
came out for an encore that shocked the advocates for affordable
housing programs: He shut down most of HUD's subsidy programs.
In the winter of 1973, as he started his second term in office (the one
that would end with his resignation), he declared a moratorium on
all housing programs.

In August 1974, a new law was passed that created the Community Development Block Grant (CDBG) program and a new system for providing housing assistance. The program merged seven
categorical programs into a block of flexible community-development
funds distributed each year by a formula that considers each locality's population and measures of distress, including poverty, age of
housing, and housing overcrowding.

The law created the Section 8 program to encourage production
of privately-owned housing for low-income households. The first component involved a housing allowance for individual households, which
provided them with the difference between what they could afford,
based on their paying 25 percent of household income (changed to 30
percent in 1981), and the market rent for a privately-owned apartment.

The second component of Section 8 continued the focus of previous programs on project-based assistance, but included technical changes to make sure subsidized properties would remain in good financial and physical shape for the long term. Most of the contracts with developers to provide housing for low-income tenants were for twenty-year terms.[13]

Awkward introductions

Under President Jimmy Carter, urban policy became an important issue again. When Carter took office as president in 1977, HUD resumed the role that Johnson intended, as a creative problem solver for cities and the poorly housed. But the renewed focus and idealism was not to last for long.

Several subsequent presidents did not share Carter's interest. They acted as if HUD did not exist. They had so little regard for the agency that they did not even remember who they appointed to run it.

Ronald Reagan saw his HUD secretary at a White House event for big city mayors and thought he was one of the mayors. George W. Bush mistakenly introduced his HUD secretary as the head of the Department of Health and Human Services. They were funny incidents, but they clearly illustrated how little Reagan and Bush cared about who was running HUD or what they were doing there.

It should come as no surprise then that under these two presidents, there were well-publicized scandals about HUD executives focusing on political patronage and self-dealing rather than housing and urban revitalization.

Under Reagan and Bush, HUD was an out-of-the-way place where presidential campaign loyalists could be rewarded if they did not merit better jobs elsewhere in the government. They were not expected to work hard at HUD, unless it was to further their own careers. They had every opportunity to use their positions to steer government contracts and grants to reward political allies and help position themselves for employment in the private sector later.

The Reagan Administration came into office promising to end waste, fraud, and inefficiency in the federal government. The appointees he selected for HUD must not have received the memo, because they wasted resources, engaged in self-dealing, and made the agency far more inefficient than it was when they came into office.

First, Reagan fired most of HUD's senior staff, terminating many more people than is usually the case at the change from one administration to another. These were people who knew the department's programs well, and it was widely believed that the terminations were intended to hurt the agency's ability to function. These senior staffers were replaced by people who earned their posts through political service to the new president, not due to their housing and community development experience.

Under Reagan's appointees at HUD, the usual practice of awarding rental housing subsidies on the basis of the quality of the projects or the need for housing did not always apply. Reagan's appointees awarded many subsidy contracts based on the political connections of the real estate developers seeking the subsidies.

Real estate companies that wanted to get subsidies would simply pay a large "consulting" fee to people who were close to the Reagan administration, including one former cabinet secretary. In return for that fee, these consultants would make sure HUD officials moved their clients to the top of the list for assistance.

A 1989 report by HUD Inspector General Paul A. Adams said awards of money for rehabilitation of older buildings to be used for affordable apartments "was based on the perception and reality of favoritism." It was estimated that prominent people connected to the Reagan administration had collected $8 million in fees for helping their clients get the subsidy contracts.

It was known as the Section 8 influence peddling scandal. The congressional investigation and a subsequent criminal investigation stayed in the news for months and damaged HUD's reputation severely.[14]

• • •

The scandal had nothing to do with the day-to-day activities of nonpolitical civil servants or the merits of the programs involved. But it struck a powerful blow to the effectiveness of the agency, and devastated the morale of its employees. It would take years for HUD to recover, partly because Congress passed a law called the HUD Reform Act. This law imposed cumbersome new restrictions on how decisions were made at the agency, creating more problems than it solved.

The poorly conceived law was still another example of how Congress excels at imposing complex procedural requirements that create delay and add cost with little benefit – but stinks at providing consistent oversight of government operations.

In this case, important members of Congress knew full well what Reagan appointees were doing at HUD for some time but did nothing to prevent it. They only took an interest when the story broke in the press, giving them the opportunity to get exposure posing as crusaders for good government.

HUD faces elimination

The next assault on HUD came 30 years after Congress authorized the agency. An up-and-coming Republican named Newt Gingrich decided that the old Southern hatred of HUD should rise again.

Republicans took control of the House of Representatives in 1995 and elected Gingrich to be speaker of the house. He made a very public point of targeting HUD for elimination.

His idea was picked up by Sen. Robert Dole when he became the Republican candidate for president that year.

Dole's explanation, in a March 10, 1995, speech, was typical of the shallow, knee-jerk nature of attacks on HUD. "Many of HUD's main programs don't even pretend to help the poor. Others just hurt them," Dole said. "They have not alleviated poverty, they have deepened it. They have not ended suffering, they have prolonged it."

It was complete nonsense, with no factual support at all and no mention of any better approaches. But Dole's offhanded dismissal of HUD and the millions of people it helps was proof that Republicans had not learned to accept the agency even 30 years after it was created.

Dole did not win, and Gingrich backed off from attacking HUD. However, the episode had a profound impact. President Bill Clinton attempted to short-circuit the Republican attack by volunteering substantial cuts to HUD's budget. HUD downsized its staff from about 13,500 to around 9,000 in 2002. It made up for the lost personnel by vastly increasing its reliance on outside contractors.

From 2002 to 2005 alone, HUD awarded contracts totaling $4.2 billion. That's $1 billion per year.

Data is not readily available on contract volume in more recent years. But the record shows that efficient results are elusive when it comes to such heavy reliance on contractors.

Under President George W. Bush, HUD secretary Alphonso Jackson publicly bragged that he would never approve a contract to go to a person who criticized the president. There were at least two investigations into contracting procedures as well as the political and personal steering of contracts by HUD staff to personal friends and business associates. No one was indicted for criminal wrongdoing, but HUD was faulted for not evaluating the work of contractors thoroughly.

It was also revealed that a large percentage of contracts were awarded without the kind of full and fair competitive bidding that would have ensured the government got the best value for its contracting dollars. This was largely due to a complex system of federal contracting preferences.

The ongoing impact of relying on contractors instead of regular staff members has not been studied, but the experience under the Bush administration and the lack of any public effort to reform the process suggests it remains an extremely inefficient process that is susceptible to manipulation and bad decision-making.

CHAPTER FOURTEEN

HUD's Greatest Hits

It's a damned good thing that Dole, Gingrich, and the 93 percent of Republican members of the House who opposed HUD's creation in 1965 did not get their way. Despite constant attacks on its effectiveness, threats to its existence, and cuts to its budgets over the years, HUD has done an amazing amount of good for this country.

There's no denying HUD has its problems, many of which are endemic to all federal agencies, and some of which are the result of political antipathy to the agency. Managing information technology is just one example. Cumbersome management processes, complex regulations, and difficulty hiring good people and motivating them are others.

But HUD's biggest weakness for the longest period of time has been its failure to generate public and political support for the work it does. The agency has never done a good job of telling Americans about what it does and the benefits it provides. The failure at branding and story telling starts with HUD's stark, modernist logo, which does nothing to communicate its mission. It extends to the larger failure to publicize the thousands of success stories HUD has made possible over 50 years.

One has to work hard to understand all the good that HUD does. But if you look back at the state of the cities and the plight of the poorly housed before HUD existed, and look at them now, after 50 years of work, you have to give this agency credit. It has done what Lyndon Johnson hoped it would do when he persuaded Congress to create it.

The tens of thousands of men and women who have staffed the agency over the last half century have worked to perfect the bedrock of American life for people of all incomes and races: good homes and healthy, safe communities.

Some factions in Congress have never appreciated that mission. But the executives, mayors, and council members who run America's cities and counties know how much HUD has done for their communities. Lower-income people who benefit from HUD assistance know what that help has meant to them and their families. Most of them are extremely grateful and will happily talk about how housing assistance turned around or even saved their lives.

Over 50 years, HUD has taken housing and urban programs out of the business of colluding with segregationists and made them a force for economic and racial integration. It has provided a lifeline for cities as they dealt with the economic impact of the flight of whites to suburban jurisdictions and, more recently, the Great Recession.

Thanks to HUD, thousands of jobs were saved or created, miles of sidewalks and sewer lines were built, and millions of homes were rehabilitated. Housing was made affordable. Local community groups were empowered to provide leadership in their neighborhoods. The list goes on and on.

From 1994 through 2014, HUD provided housing assistance to more than 35 million lower-income individuals through various direct-subsidy programs. If data were available for 1966 to 1993, the number would be much higher.

It helped many more moderate and middle-income families buy homes by insuring privately originated mortgage loans through the Federal Housing Administration. From 1934 to 2014, the FHA insured over 44 million home mortgages. It contributed greatly to the growth in the rate of homeownership from 43.6 percent of American households in 1940 to a peak near 70 percent in 2004.

HUD also established the organizational and financial infrastructure that will support American housing and community development efforts far into the future. It has facilitated creation of a whole industry of public and private organizations involved in construction, property management, community development, job creation, housing counseling, and much more.

It has nurtured the growth of successful nonprofit organizations, both those that are community based and operate in one neighborhood, as well as larger organizations that operate regionally and even nationally.

When HUD was founded in 1965, very few states had any capacity to run housing and urban programs. Now, every state has an independent agency that can issue tax-exempt municipal bonds for development of rental housing or to provide mortgage loans to home buyers, among other things. Most of these agencies got their start running HUD programs.

A detailed compilation of all HUD's programs and all that it has achieved is beyond the scope of this book. But it's important to provide a selective list of achievements that are most fundamental to the success of our cities and helpful to people with housing needs, as well as a few that point the way toward future opportunities.

Public housing

Around 1.2 million households live in public housing, and nearly two-thirds of them include seniors or people with disabilities. There are 14,000 public housing developments, located in more than 3,500 communities.

A subset of that universe of properties are family-oriented, and a number of those properties were so old and became so run down and so crime-ridden that they were defined in the late 1980s as being "severely distressed." In some cases, that was due to the fact that the projects were concentrated in low-income areas, were poorly designed, underfunded for operations and maintenance, and over-regulated by Washington.

In the 1990s, HUD started a program that would transform decaying public housing projects into vibrant mixed-income communities that offer residents a radically new way of life and a pathway to escape poverty.

The program was originally called Housing Opportunities for People Everywhere, known by the acronym HOPE. It started out under President George H. W. Bush as a way to help public housing residents take ownership of their apartments. That idea didn't go anywhere, but in 1993, a new variation on the HOPE theme was launched. It was called HOPE VI to distinguish it from previous efforts.

"We are transforming public housing projects with problems into new mixed-income communities with promise," said Andrew Cuomo, HUD secretary in the second Clinton administration. "We are making public housing a launching pad to opportunity, jobs, and self-sufficiency—instead of a warehouse trapping people in poverty and long-term dependence."

The program's goals have been realized to a large extent. HOPE VI has turned the worst public housing projects into safe, healthy communities which bring revitalization of entire neighborhoods and growth opportunities for their residents. It has provided distressed areas with exactly what its name suggests: hope.

Over the course of 15 years, 254 HOPE VI grants were awarded. They went to 132 housing agencies to demolish 96,200 public housing units and produce 107,800 new or renovated housing units, of which 56,800 would be made affordable to the lowest-income households.[15]

In addition to new buildings with modern features like energy efficiency and good security, the new communities offer social services and educational programs. Extensive effort is made to help children

A new lease on life

When Wilmina Augustin was offered a lease on a brand-new affordable apartment at Broadcreek Renaissance in Norfolk, Va., she was overjoyed. "I felt like God was right there with me," she said.

She and her two young children had been living in an emergency shelter and transitional housing after she moved out of her home to get away from an abusive relationship.

She had been earning about $20,000 a year working for a credit union, but that was not enough to rent an apartment and cover other expenses. At the peak of the recession, she was laid off. With no income and nearing the end of the time limit for staying in transitional housing, the 32-year-old faced the grim prospect of being out on the streets with her children.

Broadcreek, financed with HUD's HOPE VI program, gave her and other single mothers an opportunity to build a better life for themselves and their children. The benefits start with the joy of finally feeling safe in one's home after long periods of severe insecurity. This opens the door to self-improvement. Wilmina is working toward obtaining a bachelor's degree in human services and moving back into private housing. "I cannot wait to see what the future brings. I want to be fully self-sufficient and give my space in the property to someone else," she said.

Wilmina is one of the tens of thousands of parents who trade terrible uncertainty for a new start in life when they get to live in affordable housing. They go from scraping by in survival mode to being able to seek better jobs and begin saving money.

of the old housing projects do better in school. In some cases, the redevelopments have included construction of entirely new schools.

HUD is also working throughout its portfolio of public housing to implement programs designed to help public housing residents develop job skills and obtain employment. This is an important innovation which has the potential to help tens of thousands of young people become more productive citizens.

Moving to Work (MTW) is a demonstration program for public housing authorities that provides them the opportunity to design and test innovative, locally designed strategies that use federal dollars more efficiently, help residents find employment and become self-sufficient, and increase housing choices for low-income families. MTW gives housing agencies exemptions from many existing public housing and voucher rules and more flexibility with how they use their federal funds.

Bringing people together

Inspired by the New Urbanist movement in city planning, most HOPE VI developments replace the high-rise projects that were popular in the '40s, '50s, and '60s with low-rise developments that mix apartments and townhouses, and sometimes single-family homes.

Private developers work in partnership with nonprofit social service providers and city and state government agencies to break down the barriers between whites and blacks, affluent and poor.

In most cases, apartments for low-income households are intermingled with identical units that are leased at market-rate rents to tenants with substantial incomes. In some developments, townhouses and homes have been successfully offered for sale to middle-class buyers.

Next time you visit Chicago, take a short cab ride west from the ultra-premium shopping of Michigan Avenue to what used to be called Cabrini Green. In the 1990s, the place became fixed in Americans' minds as a social and physical disaster area. But today, thanks to HOPE VI, it's a bold experiment in bringing people of different races and incomes together into a community.

Peter Holsten worked with a missionary's zeal to replace some of the decrepit and dysfunctional high-rise public housing that was Cabrini Green into the low-rise, mixed-income housing that is North Town Village.

Holsten Real Estate Development is one of several developers that work regularly with the Chicago Housing Authority, which has been redeveloping the city's most deteriorated high-rise public housing with a substantial degree of success.

The Chicago authority (and others around the country) has worked since the late 1990s toward the goal of creating communities with people at all income levels and of all races. As Holsten honestly attests, it takes enormous effort and an intense mix of property management and social work to overcome huge cultural differences between people of very different backgrounds.

Holsten believes it's worth every bit of effort.

So does Patrick Clancey, the long-time leader of The Community Builders (TCB), a Boston-based nonprofit organization that started renovating housing for low-income occupancy in Boston the year before HUD was created. As much as any single organization in the nation, TCB shows what mission-driven housing developers can achieve by working in partnership with HUD and local governments.

A promising model

TCB has developed 320 projects and 25,000 housing units in 15 states. Its body of work includes 15 HOPE VI public housing transformations.

"The mixed-income model is what many urban neighborhoods were like 75 years ago, but today it means working hard to recreate environments where diverse people live together," said Clancy, who retired in 2014. TCB works very hard to help public housing residents improve their job skills and find jobs, while offering their children educational opportunities.

TCB staff and tenants at its properties work together to meet ambitious and measurable goals. Key goals include doubling tenants' earned incomes and cutting the high school dropout rate for young tenants by 50 percent.

The payoff comes after years of effort, Clancy added, when youths graduate from school instead of dropping out, and think about jobs and higher education instead of being lured by the toxic culture of the street. "Supporting families in mixed-income residential environments is the best anti-poverty strategy the nation can have," Clancy said.[16]

Holsten, The Community Builders, and other developers are creating modern versions of the kind of communities that made America a melting pot 100 years ago, where people of different backgrounds and incomes blended together in urban blocks, mixing housing, retail shops, and work spaces. It's a movement with exceptional potential to break down the divisions that grew so deep in the 1960s. However, it is extremely expensive to do it well, requiring billions of dollars of federal funding to make significant progress.

HOPE VI has morphed into a new program called Choice Neighborhoods, with the goal of doing similar things for all kinds of low-income housing projects, not just public housing. The idea is sound, but it remains to be seen if Congress will provide the money necessary to make it more than a token effort.

Making room for grandma

One of HUD's most successful programs produces safe, affordable apartments for low-income elders. This was done under a program called Sec. 202 – named for the number of the section in the Housing Act of 1959 by which it was authorized.

The buildings it has produced for over 50 years offer modest apartments with basic architecture. But those properties, totaling more than 400,000 units, have transformed the lives of many older Americans, most of whom get by on nothing more than Social Security.

Tenants of Sec. 202 properties are as close to being universally happy as any group of people could be. They have a ready community of peers, so they're rarely lonely and disconnected, a common problem for elders living on their own. They have well-maintained homes with security and social activities. They receive help connecting with social and health services.

Most importantly, they have economic security. They no longer have to worry that their savings will run out and they'll have to stretch their Social Security to pay for shelter as well as food, medicine, and other necessities.

The program provides all the capital needed for nonprofit groups and public housing agencies to create housing that gives elders a new lease on life.

"We want to eliminate circumstances in which persons have to make desperate choices about whether to pay the rent, buy sufficient good food, or purchase all their needed prescriptions and take them in the dosages prescribed by doctors," said Dr. Laverne Joseph, CEO of the California-based Retirement Housing Foundation, a nonprofit that builds housing for elders in 28 states, Washington, D.C., Puerto Rico, and the U.S. Virgin Islands.

Sec. 202 housing is open to households that earn no more than 50 percent of the area median income and that include at least one person who is 62 or older when they move in. Tenants pay just 30 percent of their income for rent. In most places in America, people at those income levels have no decent options in the private, unsubsidized housing market.

Thankful for housing

"When I got here, all my burdens were lifted from me," said Margarita Rey, remembering the day she found an apartment at Angelus Plaza, an apartment building in Los Angeles that was rehabilitated by the Retirement Housing Foundation, a nonprofit group, using the federal Sec. 8 program.

Before she obtained her apartment there, she had been living alone in a one-bedroom apartment that would cost well over $2,000 a month today. She was spending down her savings at a rapid rate. "It was very bleak," she said, recalling the loneliness and the fear that her savings would run out. At Angelus Plaza, she pays 35 percent of her $923 per month income, all of which is from Social Security.

"I love my apartment. I want to stay in this apartment as long as I live," she said.

Angelus Plaza opened in 1980. It is one of the largest affordable housing communities for older adults in the nation. Located in the heart of Los Angeles's historic Bunker Hill district, Angelus Plaza is within walking distance to Angel's Flight, Grand Central Market, California Plaza, Disney Concert Hall, and the Los Angeles Music Center.

The HOME Investment Partnerships Program has been one of HUD's most successful programs. Created in 1992, it gives state and local governments maximum flexibility to use federal funds to meet local needs.

The program provides an annual grant to cities and states based on a formula. The recipients get to use the program for housing activities that they identify in a comprehensive plan.

It has been used to encourage homeownership, to rehabilitate older housing, and to help make low-income housing tax credit projects work financially. Funding for HOME fluctuated between $1.5 billion and $2 billion for much of the program's history.

In Asheville, N.C., a nonprofit called Homeward Bound uses HOME money to help homeless people find permanent housing they can afford. Since Pathways to Permanent Housing began in 2006, the organization has housed over 1,188 people.

In Vermont, HOME funding is used to help community-based housing development organizations learn how to create housing in their own neighborhoods. In many other places, it is simply used to help build rental housing or help people buy homes.

HOME has assisted more than 600 communities commit to the production of nearly 1,200,000 affordable housing units, including almost 500,000 units for first-time homebuyers. In addition, HOME has assisted nearly 300,000 tenants in obtaining direct rental assistance.

Fair housing

In addition to helping create housing, HUD has helped make existing housing available without discrimination on the basis of race, gender, and other household characteristics. The extent of effort in this area has varied depending on the priorities of the president in power.

The agency's primary duty is to investigate and resolve complaints from individuals who believe they were the victims of illegal housing discrimination. It has also gone after organizations in the real estate business that it believes have business practices that are discriminatory.

Under President Clinton, enforcement was beefed up and expanded to include more oversight of how federal programs were being operated by state and local authorities. Clinton also issued an Executive Order requiring all federal agencies to affirmatively further fair housing in their programs and activities, and gave HUD responsibility for coordinating the effort.

At various times in its history, HUD has also taken an aggressive approach to getting local governments to make sure their policies on housing and community development are not discriminatory. This is part of the agency's duty to "affirmatively further fair housing" under the 1968 Fair Housing Act.

Under President Obama, HUD launched a new policy that would require a more proactive effort by local governments, saying it was necessary "to move beyond satisfying a technical reporting requirement to a new level of community planning regarding local fair housing issues."

The new policy requires every community receiving HUD assistance to conduct a thorough assessment of its challenges related to fair housing, with these goals:

1. Reduce segregation and build on the nation's increasing racial, geographic, and economic diversity.
2. Transform racially and ethnically concentrated areas of poverty into areas of opportunity.
3. Reduce disparities in access to opportunity — such as quality schools, job centers, and transit — through residential mobility and neighborhood reinvestment.
4. Narrow gaps that leave families with children, people with disabilities, and people of different races, colors, and national origins with more severe housing problems.[17]

HUD uses the leverage of potentially withholding grant funds to elicit local cooperation on fair housing, with varying degrees of success. It supports local efforts with demographic data and direct assistance to individuals to help them move out of poor areas.

Moving to Opportunity for Fair Housing (MTO) is a 10-year research demonstration that combines tenant-based rental assistance

Laying the foundation

HUD has helped establish big picture concepts that form the foundation for tremendous future progress in how we provide housing and create and sustain communities. In broad brush, it has:

- Encouraged experiments with creating mixed-income housing
- Built local capacity for long-term sustainable communities planning that encourages higher-density and transit oriented development
- Increased the capacity of community-based organizations for planning, development and finance
- Empowered state and local governments to take more responsibility and foster innovations

with housing counseling to help very-low-income families move from poverty-stricken urban areas to low-poverty neighborhoods.

Doing homeownership right

The foreclosure crisis brought a wave of criticism of government efforts to help low- and moderate-income families buy homes. But what gets less attention is the work HUD has been doing since the crisis to help people who still have trouble paying their mortgages.

This work is in addition to a long track record of awarding grants to support housing counseling organizations to help families and individuals with their housing needs and to prevent future foreclosures.

In 2015, HUD awarded more than $36 million for grants that will help 1.5 million households find housing, make more-informed housing choices, or keep their current homes.

The funding has been used to help homebuyers realistically evaluate their readiness for a home purchase, understand their financing and down payment options, and navigate what can be an extremely confusing and difficult process. Grantees also help households find affordable rental housing and offer financial literacy training to individuals and families struggling to repair credit problems that restrict their housing options.

The department also certifies individual housing counselors to make sure they are competent.

The Federal Housing Administration has been insuring mortgage loans — and thereby increasing the flow of credit to moderate-income families to buy homes — since 1934. HUD encourages all borrowers who use FHA-insured mortgage loans to undergo counseling, offering them financial incentives to do so.

Saving our cities

City and county governments all over the country rely heavily on the Community Development Block Grant (CDBG) program. The program gives local communities the flexibility to decide for themselves how best to meet their own community development needs.

From its inception in 1974 through 2014, HUD has awarded more than $144 billion in CDBG funds to state and local governments to target their own community development priorities. This funding has gone toward the rehabilitation of affordable housing, the construction of public facilities, and the creation of job growth and business opportunities.

Each year, CDBG funds are distributed to state and local governments according to population, poverty, and other housing variables. The grants have had a positive impact on the lives of millions of Americans, 95 percent of whom have low- to moderate-incomes.

This versatile program gives localities maximum flexibility on how to use the money. Some key data on what's been achieved through the program:

- From 2004 to 2013, economic development activities directly created or retained more than 421,183 permanent jobs. During the same period, more than 1.3 million homes were rehabilitated for low- and moderate-income homeowners and renters.[18]
- From 2005 to 2013, CDBG funding improved public facilities that benefitted more than 33.7 million people. These improvements assist in providing the critical elements for suitable physical environments, including sanitary water and sewer systems, safe streets and transit-ways, and improved drainage systems.
- In 2013 alone, the program allowed state and local governments to help nearly 28,000 individuals to find permanent employment or to keep the full-time jobs they had. CDBG also supported the rehabilitation of nearly 95,000 homes and financed public improvement projects that benefitted an estimated 3.3 million residents in communities from coast to coast.[19]

HUD pioneered new concepts in community development that have turned into major programs overseen by other agencies of the federal government.

One of the fundamental innovations was the use of federal tax incentives to help stimulate private investment in specific low-income parts of urban areas. This approach to economic development originated with things like Enterprise Zones and Empowerment Zones in the 1990s.

In more recent years, a system of tax incentives for specific commercial development projects — the New Markets Tax Credit Program — was administered by the Treasury Department.

The new housing crisis

Homelessness first became recognized as a serious national problem in the 1980s, and once again, it was HUD that was charged with helping.

There were no programs to shelter the homeless, even as men and women were freezing to death on the streets of the nation's capital. The need to enact new federal programs was dramatized by a group of homeless advocates, members of Congress, and celebrities who slept outside one night in March 1987 near the Capitol.

Congress created new programs to address this need, thanks largely to one of the men who slept out that night: Rep. Stewart B. McKinney, a Republican from Connecticut.

From the passage of that law through 2014, HUD awarded more than $14 billion to thousands of local housing and service programs to combat homelessness.[20] This assistance is used primarily to provide short-term emergency shelters to help people get off the streets temporarily, especially in the cold winter months.

It also provides some permanent housing where social services are provided. This combination has been very successful in reducing the number of people who are "chronically homeless." The chronically homeless are defined as 1) having health and/or substance abuse problems, and 2) having been homeless for a year or more or had at least four episodes of homelessness in the previous three years. There were 84,291 individuals experiencing chronic homelessness, according to HUD's one-day canvassing of cities across the nation on a single night in January 2014. That is a decline of 30 percent since 2007, according to HUD.[21]

HUD has also worked very closely with the U.S. Department of Veterans Affairs to help reduce the number of vets who are on the streets of our cities.

There's much more to what HUD does with smaller programs, including helping provide housing for residents of Indian reservations and tribal areas, and for people with AIDS. It also has major responsibilities for helping make sure older housing does not present a health risk to children.

CHAPTER FIFTEEN

Toward Sustainable Communities

Providing subsidies and grants is the easy part of HUD's job. The hard part is telling local governments how to do a better job of planning their communities and managing the use of their land. However, over 50 years, HUD has shown that a small federal investment in this part of its mission can yield a very good return.

HUD has encouraged good planning at the local level for most of its existence. But a funny thing happened under the leadership of Shaun Donovan, President Obama's first HUD secretary: Federal agencies concerned with our built environment started to collaborate with each other. Even more shocking, real estate developers and environmentalists started to find common ground.

For many years, different federal agencies have worked on the various elements that go into creating communities in conflict instead of in concert. The agencies in charge of housing, transportation, and the environment did not talk to each other, let alone coordinate policies and grant making.

Meanwhile, housing developers and environmentalists have been locked in heated battles about how to balance the competing interests of creating housing vs. protecting nature and limiting pollution.

Those conflicts and the confusion they brought became much more manageable thanks to a new approach to community planning championed by HUD under Obama and Donovan.

HUD's Office of Sustainable Housing and Communities awarded roughly $140 million a year for Sustainability Planning Grants to help local governments do better planning. Donovan joined top officials from the Department of Transportation and Environmental Protection Agency to form the federal interagency partnership for sustainable communities. For the first time, these agencies would work together to make sure that all the local projects they financed met a holistic set of criteria.

In the 2000s, developers and environmentalists began to see that it was a win-win solution to build housing at higher density levels. They call it "building up, not out." The more units of housing that can be built per acre of land, the less land has to be bulldozed. Better yet, if it was land in an already built-up location, it could use existing sewers, roads and other infrastructure. Development of so-called infill housing at high densities gained active support from the Sierra Club and local environmental groups.

If new high-density developments included a mix of housing, retail, and entertainment establishments, as well as places of employment, people could walk from home to their jobs and to go shopping or for an evening out. This would reduce their need to drive.

If the developments were located close to new or existing public transportation lines, even more car trips would be eliminated.

The benefits would include less expensive housing, less consumption of virgin land, less air pollution, and reduced emission of carbon, which is believed to be a cause of climate change.

Locals take charge

The beauty of HUD's new approach to planning was that the agency did not dictate to local and regional government bodies what to do with their land, as it had done in the past. It encouraged them to think in holistic ways and to cooperate regionally, but they were invited to set their own priorities for planning the future of their communities, including land use, transportation, and housing.

HUD's job was to choose the regional groups that had the best game plan, and then give them grant money to help them bring together various stakeholders to draw up those plans.

In many older metropolitan areas, the federal funding has been used to begin what some have called "sprawl repair."

In the '60s, while the ghettos were growing and cities were suffering economic decline, the U.S. government facilitated the "white flight" from those cities to the suburbs through highway construction and provision of mortgage insurance to all-white suburbs. Housing and retail development moved out farther and farther from the central cities. People commuted more and more hours by car, traffic increased, and more money was needed to keep widening our roads.

Public transit was generally neglected.

In the 1990s and 2000s, as home prices rose rapidly, aspiring home buyers were told to "drive till you qualify." The idea was that buyers could circumvent rapidly rising housing costs by buying homes that were farther and farther away from employment centers. The flaw in this strategy was that it drove up commuting costs, increased pollution and drove up traffic congestion. It also required new infrastructure.

A model for good planning

The example that many regions follow for doing good planning is Envision Utah, which conducted public values research, held over 200 workshops, and listened to more than 20,000 residents between 1997 and 1999 to help make a plan for how to handle growth while protecting the environment in Salt Lake City and the Greater Wasatch Area, including 10 counties, 88 cities and towns, and more than 150 special-service districts.

After digesting all that input, the group created the Quality Growth Strategy, which provides voluntary, locally implemented, market-based solutions. Since facilitating the Quality Growth Strategy, Envision Utah has partnered with more than 100 communities in the state to put the plan into action. One of the key goals was to increase the average number of housing units per acre of land. Another was to increase use of public transportation. On those metrics and many others, the strategy is succeeding. Thanks to HUD funding and support, many more regions will now be following Utah's lead.

The long-term goal behind sustainable communities planning is to address the damage caused by the ongoing process of suburban sprawl, including traffic congestion, pollution from long commutes, highway maintenance costs, and so on.

The economic necessity of this new way of thinking and planning was described very well by the Northeast Ohio Sustainable Communities Consortium, which is planning for the future of its 12-county region with a HUD grant.[22]

Like other regions, this area is seeing central cities lose population and jobs, leaving existing infrastructure underutilized. Meanwhile, people and jobs are moving to outlying areas, where costly new infrastructure must be built to support them.

The region will lose an average of 18 houses a day to abandonment between 2013 and 2040. That's about 177,000 homes that should be demolished over that time period, if there was money to pay for the work.

Across the region, cities are emptying out while residents flock to more thinly developed areas on the fringes, requiring new roads, sewers, power lines, and other infrastructure, the consortium reported.

"The net result, with the region's total population predicted to grow by just 94,000 people in the next 27 years, is more infrastructure and fewer people to pay for it. And that means higher taxes," the report concluded.

The consortium summed up the situation clearly:

> Suburban growth can't pay for itself without a bigger hit to taxpayers. And cities will have to pay for the cost of removing unwanted houses rendered surplus by an epidemic of decay and abandonment launched by the foreclosure crisis and the Great Recession.

HUD's planning efforts dovetail nicely with what's happening in California, Washington state, and other states. The federal government, including HUD, is not trying to tackle the issue of how much people drive and how that adds to carbon emissions that contribute to climate change. However, the states are attacking that problem directly, and it has a fascinating connection to housing.

The California Global Warming Solutions Act of 2006 requires the state to reduce greenhouse gas emissions. One way it directs that this be done is by reducing vehicle miles traveled (VMT) through more transit-oriented real estate development. The implementing mechanism for this part of the effort is Senate Bill 375.

This law requires that regions plan for more compact growth. Regional associations of governments are tasked with crafting sustainable communities strategies. The legislature included strong measures to encourage cities to zone sufficient land to meet affordable housing needs.

This strategy makes transportation spending a way to encourage higher-density, mixed-income communities instead of the main impetus driving suburban sprawl. The law gives local transportation planning agencies leverage to make funding for highway projects contingent on local performance in land use planning. It also creates a legal mechanism for developers to override local zoning if a locality will not let them build affordable housing.

To encourage developers to build in designated high-density,

transit-friendly locations, the state offers exemptions from some environmental review requirements. It's an elegant system of incentives and penalties that show great promise, although the results will
take years to realize.

How to be inclusive

One of the promising innovations that HUD encourages local
governments to adopt is a thing called "inclusionary zoning." The
idea is to offer incentives to private developers of market-rate
housing to include some affordable units in their projects.

More than 500 localities in the United States have adopted inclusionary zoning policies in some form, producing approximately
129,000 to 150,000 units nationally over 40 years, according to a
2012 study by RAND Corp.

One of the most successful such programs is operated by
Montgomery County, Md. Between 1976 and 2011, the program
produced more than 13,000 affordable housing units that have
been sold or rented to low- and moderate-income households.

HUD provides some research and advice to localities on this
approach but not much more. If the federal government used its
power to encourage more such programs, it could go a long way
to improve availability of affordable housing and spur developments that bring together residents with a range of incomes.

The most important element is that it makes an explicit connection between how local governments deal with housing needs and
the ability of those governments to obtain state and federal transportation dollars. It's an approach that could easily be a model for many
other states, and even the federal government.

More recently, California has taken still another step toward a
progressive approach to housing and the environment. It is dedicating
some of the money from the auctioning of carbon emission rights to be
used to finance affordable housing that is located near public transit.

Allowing affordable housing

Sometimes, HUD has to go beyond just facilitating the local planning
process to taking direct action to change local policies. When a local

government is especially determined to use its land-use policies to prevent construction of affordable housing, HUD can withhold grant money which that jurisdiction would otherwise receive under the mandate of the Fair Housing Act to "affirmatively further fair housing."

The department doesn't do it often, but when it does, it sends a clear message to localities everywhere that it is not okay to use land-use and building regulations to keep people of color out of their communities by blocking construction of housing they can afford.

In 2009, HUD won a major battle of wills over this issue with the government of Westchester County, N. Y.

Located just to the north of New York City, it is home to many executives who commute to Manhattan. The median income of county residents in 2011 was $77,006.

No room for waiters

The affluent county offers thousands of jobs for waiters, cooks, busboys, maids, gardeners, and other service personnel. A large proportion of these workers commute to their jobs from the Bronx, Queens, and Brooklyn, the boroughs of New York City where there is still some relatively affordable housing. They could not afford homes or apartments in Westchester, and the local governments that make the rules on housing construction were just fine with that.

The various local governments in Westchester were so effective at keeping affordable housing out that HUD finally decided to take a stand. HUD gave Westchester County's government a choice: Either make affordable housing construction happen soon, and market those homes to people of color, or lose federal community development grant money.

The dispute ended up in court. Andrew Spano, the chief executive of the county at the time, agreed to expedite development of 750 units of affordable housing in predominantly white communities in the county of nearly 1 million people and to market the housing as HUD directed.

In the first five years after the 2009 settlement, 173 units had been built according to HUD's wishes. More units were in the works, but they were moving very slowly through local land-use and building-permit processes.

A case in point is Chappaqua Station, a proposed apartment development in Chappaqua, a small town about 90 minutes north of New York City.

The affluent area is home to some very prominent Democratic political leaders, including Bill and Hillary Clinton as well as Andrew Cuomo, governor of New York State.

The proposed development would have 28 apartments. But even that small amount of housing was too much.

The town council repeatedly debated the location of the property, its size, its design and almost everything else you could imagine. A change in the council's composition brought an explicit determination to kill the project. Although that effort had not succeeded as of 2015, it had taken five years of struggle and added substantial cost to the project.

Hillary Clinton has not taken a position on whether the 28 apartments should be built or not. Bill Clinton was asked if he supported the development plan. He refused to take a position. Over five years of debate, no one in a position of power or prestige in the area has spoken out in favor of the development.

• • •

If the developer perseveres and finally gets to build, it will cost around 50 percent more than it should due to the opposition. As of mid-2014, the developer had spent at least $1.5 million to satisfy every request and requirement the townspeople had raised. That comes out to $53,000 per unit.

That bears repeating. That $53,000 in added costs for one new apartment is just to deal with all the roadblocks to obtaining a building permit. It doesn't include the cost of land or construction. And that was the preliminary total. It could cost the developer, and the state of New York, which is subsidizing the project, as much as $75,000 extra per unit by the time the townspeople finish erecting obstacles to construction.

That would have been enough to buy a median-priced, new, single-family home in America 25 years ago. Even today in New York State, it would be enough to buy a manufactured home.

Meanwhile, the people who bus the tables and clean the houses in the affluent community will continue to have to live in places like the South Bronx.

Their only hope is for HUD to persevere in pushing places like Westchester to make housing happen.

As long as the president in power supports HUD's efforts, it will keep trying to break down barriers to affordable housing development. But if the next president doesn't choose to do that, the people who commute long distances to their jobs to places like Chappaqua can only dream of having the same community benefits that the children of their employers enjoy.

• • •

The struggle over where affordable housing should be built frequently ends up in court. Sometimes the U.S. Department of Justice takes independent action, filing lawsuits when it believes a local government's policies have a "disparate impact" on minorities and can be challenged under the Fair Housing Act.

The battle is extremely important because if affluent communities are allowed to prevent construction of affordable apartments, government-assisted housing often ends up being located in communities that have lower-income populations and large numbers of affordable units already. State and federal agencies see this as following the "path of least resistance" to getting housing built, since these communities don't have the political or financial ability to fight new developments.

However, communities in this position have begun to resist. In 2015, a nonprofit organization in Dallas went all the way to the U.S. Supreme Court with a complaint that the Texas Department of Housing and Community Affairs has concentrated its development of affordable housing in areas mainly populated by minorities. The Inclusive Communities Project (ICP) is a not-for-profit organization in Dallas that works for the creation and maintenance of racially and economically inclusive communities. It believes that government programs should be used to give low-income families the opportunity to live throughout the metro area, not just in low-income neighborhoods.

ICP's mission statement says that it "envisions an America where equality is created and sustained in the community through access to good schools, affordable housing, safe neighborhoods, and economic opportunity."

Giving children a chance

Why does HUD go to so much trouble to make sure housing is available to lower income families in affluent suburban communities? One important reason is that a good education is critical to breaking

The Rosa Parks of Affordable Housing

State governments have joined HUD in pursuit of a more level playing field for affordable housing development. New Jersey is one of the states with a strong legal tradition of enabling housing sponsors to challenge local governments that refuse to permit such housing.

The legal principle involved in the Garden State is called the "Mt. Laurel doctrine," and got its start when a black woman named Ethel R. Lawrence got upset because her children could not afford housing in Mt. Laurel, N.J., where she had raised them.

Lawrence is known as the Rosa Parks of affordable housing. She was concerned that her children, along with other black households, could not find homes that were affordable and in sound condition. She challenged the town government for its policy of allowing only construction of high-priced housing, joining in litigation brought by civil rights groups that resulted in two New Jersey Supreme Court decisions that stopped towns from shutting out the poor through exclusionary zoning.

The Mount Laurel legal doctrine has had a powerful impact across the state of New Jersey. It has been used as the legal leverage necessary to get localities to open their land to affordable housing development. It has resulted in the development of 60,000 homes affordable to lower-income households, according to Peter O'Connor, of Fair Share Housing Development in New Jersey.

Recently, Gov. Chris Christie urged the state Supreme Court to reverse its position on exclusionary zoning. The court refused to do so. But it's only a matter of time till another legal assault is launched.

"A failed social experiment." That's what Christie called the Mt. Laurel doctrine. The tens of thousands of New Jersey residents who get to live in nice communities because of it would disagree.

the cycle of intergenerational poverty.

We are making progress in improving inner city schools but it has been painfully slow. That's why one of the goals of housing policy has been to reduce segregation of housing by income and race.

Housing and zoning policies determine where people with lower incomes can afford to obtain housing. In most cases, the location of one's home determines what school one may attend. The better the school, the better a kid's chances in life.

"Where you live matters to economic mobility," said Erin Currier, who directs Pew Research Center's economic mobility research. "Neighborhoods play an important role in determining a family's prospects of moving up the economic ladder, which is especially important since a majority of metro areas have become more economically segregated over time."

The Bipartisan Policy Center, a Washington, D.C., group that brings together Republican and Democratic government officials, seconded that conclusion in a recent report on housing needs:

> Affordable housing strategies that help low-income families access low-poverty neighborhoods or communities with high-performing schools can contribute to positive educational outcomes. Better educational performance, in turn, may lead to greater employment opportunities, higher incomes, and a boost to national wealth and productivity.[23]

CHAPTER SIXTEEN

A Forbidding Future

The outlook for housing and community development in America can be summarized in four words: More need, fewer resources.

When the cities erupted in violence after Martin Luther King's death in 1968, the American population was 200 million. By 2006, it had grown to 300 million.

The Census Bureau projects that the U.S. population will grow by 80 million people by 2050, and estimates are that at least 80 percent of that growth (over 60 million people) will come in urban areas.

Much of the growth has been and will be among people of color.

Minority households will account for 7 out of 10 new households formed between 2013 and 2023, according to "The State of the Nation's Housing 2013" from Harvard's Joint Center for Housing Studies. That's 8.7 million new households in 10 years.

Looking out a bit further, the black population is expected to increase from 41.2 million to 61.8 million from 2010 to 2060.

The Hispanic population is expected to more than double, from 53.3 million in 2012 to 128.8 million in 2060. Consequently, by the end of the period, nearly one in three U.S. residents would be Hispanic, up from about one in six today.

If you factor in the growth of the elderly population, you quickly see that the divisions in America will be multifaceted. They will no longer be just about race but income, ethnicity, and age as well.

The 85-and-older population will grow to close to 9 million by 2020. As the baby boom generation pushes into old age, the number of those over 85 will hit 14.2 million in 2040, according to census data compiled by the U.S. Administration on Aging.

These trends are invisible to most members of Congress. The mere mention of demographic projections sends most of them into an apathy coma. Spending money today to head off problems tomorrow is not what helps them raise money and win votes.

But just hypothetically, if a handful of legislators did care, they'd see two problems with the population growth projections. First, there is little chance new housing construction will keep up with overall demand. Second, the housing that will be constructed will be too expensive for a large proportion of the minority population, the elderly, and all people with low incomes.

Many of the growing number of elders will depend on Social Security as their primary source of income, and it won't be enough to pay for market-rate housing in most places, at least not for apartments that are safe and clean. Our low-income elders will be living in a new kind of ghetto: the decaying districts where old people live in squalor, waiting to die.

Some of the growing numbers of minority households will be prosperous enough to find housing in relatively affluent areas, but many of them will not. The median income of minority households fell 9 percent, from $37,100 in 2010 to $33,600 in 2013, according to the Federal Reserve Board.[24] Even people earning at or above that level will find it hard to cover the cost of new housing being built almost anywhere in America.

These less affluent households will have to rely on the supply of older, poorly located, or substandard housing, a supply which is shrinking year by year due to obsolescence and demolition.

Private housing production

When Congress passed the 1965 housing act, it understood that federal subsidy programs alone would not be enough to provide affordable housing for our growing population.

Congress recognized then, when housing costs were so much lower, that local land-use and building policies and regulations would result in a steady escalation of costs. These increases affect every single unit of housing built in America, whether it is a privately financed home for sale to the middle class or rental housing for working people.

The law was clear about the need to encourage local property owners and private companies to meet a large part of the total housing need. It directed the federal government to study state and local housing and building laws, standards, codes and regulations, and their impact on housing costs, to see how they could be simplified, as well as state and local zoning and land-use laws to find ways to obtain further growth and development

Congress recognized the absurdity of a situation in which housing agencies used federal funding to build as much affordable housing as possible, while zoning and building departments in the same communities drove up housing costs by making more and more costly demands on each new development.

But as absurd as that may seem, it is exactly what is happening all over America. Different parts of state and local governments continue to work at cross-purposes, some trying to subsidize housing and others trying to make it more expensive. In most communities, these competing functions work independently with little adherence to any overall strategy on housing.

When the law was passed, new housing could be constructed with rents and prices that were affordable for people earning the median income in their areas. Not anymore. Now, in almost every corner of our nation, the only properties being built are for upper middle class or high-income households.

Failed vision

Congress also said we should use federal state and local tax policies to create incentives to build housing and make improvements to existing structures. The problem was that Congress never said exactly how that would happen, and it never gave HUD any specific power to do anything about local land-use and building regulations and fees. The courts generally sided with local authorities whenever there was a challenge to their power to regulate construction any way they wanted.

The federal government has many tools to work with, from the ability to withhold federal housing and highway funds to its control of the tax treatment of city and county municipal bonds. But it has not used its powers to make progress on this issue. Local governments still have carte blanche to keep the cost of housing high and prevent development of subsidized homes or apartments.

Part of the problem is that the politics of housing have always favored homeownership. Rental housing in multifamily structures is the most efficient way to provide housing, but it is also the least popular with local governments, and federal policy has tended to echo that perception.

Republicans have traditionally taken the lead on the issue of reducing the cost burden caused by local regulation of housing.

In the past, when the party bothered to draft a housing platform at all, it usually said that we could not afford to keep spending more and more taxpayer money to subsidize housing for the poor. It balanced that with recognition that something had to be done to stem the relentless cost increases for privately financed housing by reducing the inflationary impact of local land-use and building regulations on housing.

Republicans have acted on the first part of that platform by cutting HUD housing spending. But they have done almost nothing about the second part: reducing housing costs. Democrats don't buy into the Republican ideology of deregulation and don't want to challenge local regulatory authority. As a result, HUD does very little to push for the local deregulation of housing.

In an era when the federal government gets involved in monitoring almost every aspect of our lives, its lack of concern for housing costs is actually quite remarkable. Even after the foreclosure crisis, the focus in Washington was entirely on lending practices and never even touched on the incredible explosion of home sales prices that made the market overheat.

Federal statutes require that every federal agency issuing a new rule evaluate how much paperwork it would require. But there's no obligation on any agency issuing a new rule to think about the impact it would have on housing costs.

Environmental impact statements are required for thousands of projects, but there is no such thing as a "housing cost impact" study at the state or federal level.

Until our national political leaders find the nerve to address this problem, housing costs will keep rising. Meanwhile, Congress will keep slicing and dicing appropriations for housing programs, and helping fewer and fewer people even as the need grows ever larger.

• • •

A major transition in housing policy in the 1970s and 1980s was to switch from the provision of buildings dedicated for use as affordable housing to the distribution of vouchers that were good for a large part of the rent on any privately owned rental housing unit that an eligible person wished to occupy.

Tenants who qualify for Housing Choice Vouchers and wait long enough to receive assistance pay only 30 percent of their income for rent on modest apartments that meet government standards for rent levels and condition. The government pays the difference between what the tenant can afford and what the landlord charges.

The program has been very effective in encouraging mobility, since voucher holders can rent apartments outside of areas where poverty and dedicated affordable housing is concentrated.

But it faces two serious problems:

First, it provides an open-ended housing subsidy without connecting those who receive help to any social services intended to help them improve their education or employment situation.

Second, it is getting harder to use vouchers because their utility depends on the level of market-rate rents in the private market. Rents for privately owned housing are rising to such an extent that it's getting harder for voucher holders to find units they can afford, even with the help of the vouchers.

On the chopping block

The political animosity toward HUD and its programs goes on display every spring, when Congress starts the ritual of the annual federal budgeting process. Federal spending on HUD programs peaked in the 1970s and has been steadily declining since then. Depending on the outcome of the 2016 presidential election, the worst may be yet to come.

The Housing and Urban Development Act of 1968, which is still on the books, said it was our national goal to create 600,000 units of affordable housing per year. We came close to meeting that goal under President Jimmy Carter.

Then, in 1983, President Ronald Reagan decided we should stop financing construction of new rental housing under the Sec. 8 program. Congress went along with Reagan's wishes, and the era of government subsidies for large scale new construction of affordable housing that had started in 1937 was over.

"The whole attitude that the federal government can solve all the housing problems of this country—those days are over," said one of Reagan's top appointees at HUD.

Under Reagan, a new program was created to finance construction of apartments through the use of tax incentives. It was called

the Low-Income Housing Tax Credit (LIHTC), and it has survived
the political attacks on housing programs through the 2015 publication of this book.

Housing finance agencies in all 50 states, plus the District of
Columbia, Puerto Rico, and the Virgin Islands, used tax credits to
finance three million affordable rental homes from 1987 through
2014, according to the National Council of State Housing Agencies.
That comes out to about 110,000 units a year, or about one-sixth of
the annual production that Congress said was necessary.

The tax-credit program provides a very shallow subsidy. That
means it allows housing to be built, but only at rents that are generally only slightly lower than rents for existing market-rate housing. It
only serves poor households when it is combined with additional government subsidies, and most sources of such subsidies are shrinking.

A select list of major federal programs that have been eliminated
entirely:

- New construction of public housing
- New construction of housing for low-income elders (Sec.
  202)
- New construction of privately owned affordable apartments
  (Sec. 8)
- HOPE VI reconstruction of existing public housing
- Grants for sustainable community planning

In addition, the program relies heavily on private real estate investors and developers. This has a dual benefit: it brings the exper-
tise of the private sector to bear on the challenge of development and
housing management. It also creates a powerful and wealthy political constituency for the program. However, it also means the housing
it produces is often very expensive.

In the 1970s, federal subsidies produced 20,000 low-cost apartments per year for elders and people with handicaps under Sec. 202.
In 2002, the Commission on Affordable Housing and Health Facility
Needs for Seniors in the 21st Century told Congress that we needed
to build 40,000 units per year just to house the growing numbers of
low-income elders.[25]

In 2011, Congress decided to stop providing any funds for construction of new housing for elders. Instead of ramping up production to meet the needs of an aging population, Congress reduced production to zero.

Although more than $380 million was provided in 2014, it was all allocated for modifying and supporting existing buildings, not for constructing new apartments.

Earlier in this book, there is a section about the great success of the HOPE VI program. That program provided an incredible return on taxpayer funds. The $6 billion HUD invested in HOPE VI leveraged $17.5 billion in direct investment from private capital sources and state and local governments.

No dollar value has been attached to the larger social benefits it provided, both in terms of the improved employment prospects for residents and the reduced cost to localities for dealing with the crime and other problems that were substantially reduced after redevelopment. Those benefits, if measured, would probably double or triple the total return on taxpayers' money over time.

So, did Congress extend the program to more communities troubled by the consequences of concentrated poverty? No. It terminated it. Back in 2010, HUD made its last grants under the program.

A new program was enacted to do what HOPE VI did, but for a larger universe of apartment buildings. The Choice Neighborhoods Program was funded at only $90 million for 2014. Considering that each neighborhood transformation it aims to create requires $20 million or more in federal funds, that appropriation won't go very far.

HUD requested $400 million for 2014. Congress provided less than 25 percent of that. For housing and urban programs, it's a very familiar story. The next step is predictable. Congress will say the program is not having a large enough impact and will use that as its excuse to terminate it.

Preservation of existing housing

The mathematics of housing funding revolve around how many low-income households can be assisted by HUD in any given year. The debate used to be about how much we could increase the number of households that received housing help each year. Now it's usually about how much of a reduction will be required each year from the numbers assisted in the previous year.

This occurs even when funding levels are held steady because of the increasing cost of housing. When funding levels are cut and costs rise, the declines are more extreme.

The number of very-low-income renters that are eligible for federal rental assistance increased from 15.9 million in 2007 to 19.3 million in 2011. That's an increase of more than 3 million people. But only 23.8 percent of the people in need received federal housing assistance that year. That's down from 27.4 percent in 2007, according to Harvard University's Joint Center for Housing Studies.

The percentage of needy people who actually get help will almost certainly continue to decline. Even with consistent levels of appropriations from Congress and state governments, which is never a given, the number of people who can be assisted continues to decline because of the increasing cost of housing.

There was a temporary surge in spending under the economic stimulus legislation of 2009 for several housing and urban programs. But once that was gone, and Republicans took control of the House of Representatives, a new wave of budget cuts was unleashed on all domestic programs, including housing and urban programs.

Budget cuts accelerate

Nondefense discretionary (NDD) programs comprise domestic and international programs outside of national defense that Congress funds on an annual basis. NDD spending includes all of the assistance offered by HUD because none of that aid is legally mandated to be provided. It is discretionary, as opposed to programs like Medicare, which is an entitlement program, meaning everyone who is eligible definitely receives assistance.

Spending on NDD programs peaked in the late 1970s at 5 percent of gross domestic product (GDP). It declined to 3 percent in the late 1990s, surged briefly in 2010, and then headed downward again. The Center on Budget and Policy Priorities (CBPP) projects it will drop to 2.5 percent by 2022.

This projected drop is largely due to the future effects of the 2011 Budget Control Act (BCA), which set limits, or "caps," on annual discretionary funding through 2021. It imposes separate caps for defense and nondefense funding. In addition, the BCA mandated automatic further reductions – called "sequestration" – after Congress failed to adopt a more comprehensive deficit-reduction plan.

It would be bad enough if we were only dealing with a decline in the number of new households that receive housing assistance every year. But it's worse than that. Thousands of low-income people who have been residing in subsidized housing are being thrown out on the streets due to federal budgets and policies.

New construction of public housing was terminated years ago. But the budget cutters are still targeting the program by cutting federal funding that local housing authorities use for management, upkeep, and repairs.

Loss of housing

Given the advanced age of most public housing buildings, decreased capital funding for replacement of major systems and subsidies for maintenance, security, and operations have a very obvious result: the deterioration and loss of public housing units. That suits the budget cutters just fine, because once a project is abandoned and demolished, it needs no more federal support.

These cuts amount to "slow death by attrition," according to The Bipartisan Policy Center. The consistent shortfall in funding "wastes valuable federal housing assets and risks the loss of both high-quality and deteriorating units alike. In addition, it penalizes residents."

More than 165,000 public housing units have been demolished or otherwise removed from the stock without being replaced, according to CBPP.

The ongoing loss of public housing is estimated to be 10,000 units per year, largely for lack of funds to make necessary repairs, according to the "State of the Nation's Housing" report from Harvard's Joint Center for Housing Studies.

Budget austerity is also affecting people living in privately owned buildings that provide dedicated affordable housing under the Sec. 8 subsidy program.

These programs depend on the willing participation of private owners who sign contracts with the federal government to make the housing available to lower-income people for specific periods of time.

Over the past two decades, increasing numbers of owners have decided not to renew those contracts. That means the housing ceases to be available for poor households.

Between 10,000 and 15,000 units of affordable Sec. 8 housing were being lost every year as property owners exited the program, according to a 2013 report by CBPP.

More than 190,000 units could be lost over the next decade, according to Harvard's Joint Center on Housing Studies. That's on top of the tens of thousands that were already lost before this book went to press.

One of the favorite targets for budget cutters is the Community Development Block Grant program, the most widely used and most flexible tool HUD has to help cities.

In 2005, President George W. Bush proposed eliminating the CDBG program. A massive lobbying effort by the nation's mayors saved it from elimination, but not from deep budget cuts. In 2010, the CDBG appropriation was $4.45 billion. In 2011, it was reduced to $3.5 billion. In 2012 through 2014, it had dropped to a little over $3 billion per year.

The reduction of roughly $1.4 billion in CDBG funding since 2010 has "significantly undermined projects and shuttered services that cities need to create jobs for our residents and that drive economic growth throughout our communities," according to the National League of Cities.

For fiscal year 2014, the Republican majority in the House of Representatives proposed cutting CDBG funding to just $1.6 billion. The cut did not become law. However, it is highly likely that opponents of the program will try again to slash it, if not kill it.

With funding at the federal and state levels that used to go to cities being systematically eliminated, more and more of the burden is being put on the backs of municipal governments that don't have the resources to make up for the cuts, said Ed Pawlowski, mayor of Allentown, Pa.

In Allentown and other cities without strong economic growth, there is little potential to make up for the cuts in federal and state funding by raising local taxes, Pawlowski added.

He and other mayors warn of a downward spiral: the less cities have to spend on keeping their neighborhoods and downtowns in good shape, the harder it is to attract the investment and jobs that help them expand their tax base and maintain economic viability.

Who gets subsidies?

Some politicians love to play on the feeling among middle-class voters that HUD housing assistance goes to people who don't deserve the help, while millions of middle-class Americans receive no government assistance at all.

It's a matter of opinion who deserves assistance and who doesn't, but it's a matter of fact who gets it and who doesn't.

The poor don't get any more help with housing than middle- and upper-income Americans. On the contrary, higher income groups generally get more help.

The federal government subsidizes people who buy homes by allowing them to deduct the interest on their mortgages and the local property taxes on their homes from income when they figure their taxes. These are called tax expenditures, and the cost is the amount of tax revenue that is lost to the government due to the deductions.

These subsidies are not as obvious as the ones offered to poor tenants, because they come through the tax code, but they are just as real.

While the amount of subsidies offered through HUD to lower-income people is strictly limited, homeownership tax breaks are extremely generous, and politically very well defended by the home construction, sales, and finance industries.

Homeowners who itemize on their tax returns can deduct the interest paid on mortgages on first and second homes up to a total mortgage amount of $1 million. They can deduct the property taxes they pay to local governments for any number of homes with no limit.

No tax on profits

Those incentives were generous enough. Then, in 1997, Congress expanded a previous incentive to make it far more generous. The expanded provision allows owners to avoid paying federal tax on the profit they make when they sell their homes. At first it was limited to people over 55 or people who were putting the profits toward a new, more expensive home.

Now it can be used multiple times by people of all ages to avoid all taxes on $250,000 in gain for singles and $500,000 in gain for couples. That means that most people can buy and sell homes for significant gains without paying any federal taxes at all.

The mortgage interest deduction was expected to reduce federal revenues by $70 billion in 2013 and by $379 billion over the five years from 2013 to 2017, according to the Joint Committee on Taxation (JCT).[26]

The cost of the state and local property tax deduction was $16.4

billion. The cost in lost revenue of the exemption from taxation on capital gains on owner-occupied housing was $15.3 billion.

Total it all up, and federal tax expenditures for homeowners of all income levels are right around $100 billion per year. That's more than twice as much as what was appropriated directly for all HUD programs in a typical recent year, including housing, community development, administration, fair housing enforcement, regulatory functions, and research.

This is not to say homeownership is not a good thing to promote for all Americans. It is. But these tax deductions favor affluent people over those with lower incomes. They also reduce the ability of the federal government to appropriate more money to subsidize rental housing for lower-income families.

The tax benefits for homeownership have no targeting or income limits. More than three-fourths of the value of the mortgage interest and property tax deductions goes to households with incomes of more than $100,000. Close to a third goes to families with incomes above $200,000. That's according to estimates by the JCT.

Most low and moderate income Americans rent their homes, and very few of them get government assistance to help them keep a roof over their heads.

As noted earlier in this book, less than 25 percent of poor households receive any help from the government to pay their rent. However, 100 percent of those who itemize their tax returns and own homes can claim the homeownership tax breaks, regardless of their income.

Who gets help

Looking at tax expenditures as well as direct subsidies for housing, more than 75 percent of federal housing spending in 2012 went to homeowners, according to the Center on Budget and Policy Priorities. Renters received less than one-fourth of federal housing subsidies despite making up more than a third of households, said Barbara Sard, vice president for housing policy at the CBPP.

Renters get no breaks on their taxes for any portion of what they pay in rent, even though a substantial part of that rent goes toward paying the interest costs and property taxes for the building in which they reside.

Blacks and Hispanics are less likely to be homeowners than whites, so they don't have the same chance to participate in these tax benefits. In addition, these tax breaks are of no use to households that own their home but do not itemize their tax returns. This is the case for many less-affluent families, but is rarely true for households with higher incomes.

The amount that should be directly appropriated for housing assistance is subject to intense debate during the annual Congressional budget process. Cuts in funding are made frequently. However, the tax breaks for homeownership grow steadily without any review or discussion about whether they are too costly.

The annual tax expenditure for the three homeownership tax breaks is projected to increase to $178 billion in 2018.[27]

If these tax breaks were curtailed, some portion of that $168 billion could be spent to help poor families obtain housing or maintain the older rental housing that constitutes our only private-market options for many people.

CHAPTER SEVENTEEN

Conclusion

In the mid-1960s, the need for extensive federal housing and urban development programs, and an agency to run them, was as clear as the wailing of sirens on police cars responding to riots in America's inner cities.

Now, as the Department of Housing and Urban Development turns 50 years old, it's an open question whether it will survive much longer. It has few allies with political power in Congress. It doesn't have any name recognition or support among voters. Its programs are perennial targets for budget cutters. Even Democratic politicians don't put up much of a fight to defend the agency.

After relentless attacks on funding for its programs, a change in power in Washington could bring complete elimination of one or more of its most critical programs. And if that were to happen, it's easy to see Congress taking the next step and finally killing off the agency.

It would be a terrible mistake if that were to happen.

But it would also be a form of slow death if a future president borrows a page from Ronald Reagan and stocks HUD with political cronies with little management ability, no vision, and a very loose and self-serving idea of public integrity.

We need HUD to not only exist but to be treated as an important part of the government with political support and strong leadership.

It is the only federal agency that focuses on the needs of our cities, especially the older industrial towns with declining economies and decaying infrastructure. It is the primary source of effort to solve our shortage of affordable housing, and the still-lingering problem of housing discrimination.

If it gets the right leadership, HUD is the only force that could possibly break down barriers to affordable housing development in suburban communities and break up the urban concentrations of poverty that have been our factories of inequality for much of the last century.

As HUD turns 50, we must not give in to apathy or denial about the problems it was created to solve – or the short attention spans that make policy discussions so unpopular in the era of tweets and twits.

We need to demand that our political and civic leaders take a new look at HUD, why it was created, what it has achieved, and what it could accomplish in its next 50 years. We need to think as boldly as Martin Luther King and Robert Kennedy did in the early '60s.

We need to visualize what our communities will look like in 2065, when HUD will be 100 years old. How will the current patterns of separation by race and income change if there is less federal government intervention? How will those trends affect the degree of inequality in our society, not to mention our cost for criminal justice, incarceration, and social programs?

What can we do now to create a better future, and what needs to change at HUD, in federal policy on local land-use powers, and at the local level?

This is about far more than the fate of a single federal agency or the bureaucrats who run it. It is about the unfinished business of dealing with racial segregation and concentration of poverty.

There was strong opposition to having an urban agency in the first place, and today there is opposition to its continued existence.

There was even stronger opposition to federal enforcement of fair housing policies for many years. It is still with us, even if it's less obvious. Today's segregationists have many guises, and their aims are not discussed openly in public, but they still have a powerful impact on our society.

Supporting HUD is a critical step in confronting and counteracting the forces working for MORE separation of Americans by race and income, not less.

Most of all, it's about finally coming to grips with the enormous and growing gap between the incomes of average Americans and what it costs to obtain housing in places where it is safe to raise families and where decent employment and educational opportunities exist.

• • •

Several best-selling books have been written on the growing inequality in America, prompting much discussion. But that conversation has generally focused on macroeconomics, glossing over the fact that the area in which a person lives matters very much to his or her ability to move up the economic ladder.

This book was written to amplify the few academic voices that are saying, "place matters." Areas of concentrated poverty are traps. They are far harder to escape than most of the readers of this book will ever know.

Where a person lives makes a huge difference in his or her ability to progress in life, especially for younger people.

HUD has done good work to improve the quality of life in the inner cities and inner suburbs and to provide housing, to the extent Congress has given it resources and presidents have given it leadership and competent management.

But the far-sighted leaders of the '60s were quite vehement about the other major requirement for responding to the terrible conditions that led to the riots of 1965 to 1968. They said we needed to make sure that lower-income people had opportunities to move to affordable housing in communities throughout our metro areas, including the suburbs, which remain mostly wealthy and white.

A series of commissions, congressional committees, and individual leaders could foresee that the longer we waited to do that work, the harder it would be, the more entrenched racial and income divisions would become, and the higher the indirect costs of conflict and dysfunction would become.

They were absolutely right. Their predictions are coming true.

HUD has tried to advance residential mobility, but with very limited tools and very limited political support.

As a nation, we never committed ourselves to long-term, sustained efforts to break down the patterns of land use that have perpetuated residential segregation by race and income. We allowed housing costs to become a one-way street that only went up.

Instead, Congress staged very time-consuming political fights every year over whether to cut levels of assistance to needy people by dollar figures that amount to rounding errors in the federal budget.

There are some local governments that understand the need for diversity and affordable housing. But there are many more that don't, and there are many thousands of activists working to make sure they never do. In some parts of the country, a politician need only suggest that affordable housing could be constructed, and he or she will be voted out of office or recalled promptly.

So, while economists debate macroeconomic solutions to rising inequality, the dynamics of place keep on working every single day. With housing costs constantly rising relative to incomes, it keeps getting harder to create affordable housing that gives less-affluent people opportunities to move to better places. Concentrations of poverty continue to hold people down.

You might call it the "geography of disadvantage."

• • •

The good news is that tremendous progress has been made, and much greater advances for more people ARE within reach – if we have the political will to seek them.

Under the first term of Barack Obama's presidency, HUD Secretary Shaun Donovan said HUD was trying to create a new "geography of opportunity." It was a great way to encapsulate the agency's purpose. That mission is at the core of why HUD was created, and it's the main reason the agency must survive and be given new capabilities.[28]

Thanks largely to HUD, we have 50 years of experience and hundreds of great examples, from new, mixed-income, mixed-use communities to the complete redevelopment of the worst of the old public housing high-rises, complete with new schools and enrichment opportunities for poor children.

We have paid our dues, and we know what works and what doesn't. We have built an infrastructure of developers, financiers, and highly professional state and local government agencies that can all work together to get good results.

We have proven that taxpayer investment in housing and urban vitality pays many dividends. It makes people and families more productive and self-sufficient; it strengthens our economy; it builds social cohesion; and it saves money on the construction of new developments on greenfields while existing neighborhoods rot.

The federal government has learned how to facilitate local innovation and enlist private capital in the effort to help people obtain good housing and create jobs in low-income areas.

HUD's predecessor agencies were often accessories to segregationists and helped them achieve their goal of racial separation. After decades of very intensive lobbying by people like Robert Weaver and Walter Mondale (to name just two), HUD gradually got more power to work on reducing segregation and discrimination.

It's hard work with limited resources, but it's worth every bit of effort because it does make a huge difference in people's lives.

• • •

To convince the next Congress to stop hacking away at spending on HUD programs, voters need to make their voices heard saying that the people and places HUD serves DO matter.

It takes a great deal of money to address the needs of high-poverty neighborhoods and today's ghettos. It is enormously expensive to build new housing affordable to the poor and to maintain the apartment buildings our government has already built at very substantial cost to American taxpayers.

Getting Congress to recognize the true cost of doing an effective job with housing and urban programs is our first priority.

However, to help more people for a much longer time, we must break down the barriers to creation of affordable housing. This can be done in dozens of ways, such as allowing second units on lots that already have one single family home, allowing more locations for manufactured housing communities, increasing allowable housing density, simplifying building codes, and much more.

The federal government must give localities a push – and give their elected officials political cover – to accelerate progress on this front.

The policy fashion of the last few years has been to get local governments to work together on a regional basis and "break down silos," in the bureaucratic vernacular. President Obama has personally encouraged this.

That's all good. But what no one in Washington wants to talk about is the real-world political challenges of acting on the many good ideas and plans that have been drawn up, especially putting money on the table to make real change happen.

State and local elected officials will attend meeting after meeting to talk about ideas. Where they have a problem is defying their voters to actually change policies that perpetuate the status quo and to create more housing opportunities.

That's where you come in. After you finish this book, let the people who represent you know you care about these issues.

If you are a millennial looking toward your own transition from

the bohemian life of a dorm or shared apartment to property ownership, remember that you have the power to shape the communities
in which you live — now and for the rest of your life.

The baby boom generation used to claim it was different than
the generation that went before it in regard to race relations. But
most of the boomers chose property appreciation over social justice.
When they would learn that affordable housing was planned for an

Guns vs. Butter

Back in the '60s, political pundits used to talk about the choice of
guns versus butter. "Guns" was shorthand for spending billions
of dollars on nuclear weapons to contain the Soviet Union and
to wage war against communism in Southeast Asia. "Butter"
was shorthand for caring for the poor and spending money on
domestic programs.

This book is not about conspiracy theories or random specula-
tion on who really killed the Kennedy brothers and Martin Luther
King, Jr.

But, one cannot write about the events of the '60s without noting
that the killing of all three men was the surest action any person
or group could have taken to make certain the nation chose guns
over butter.

All three men were dedicated to ending U.S. involvement in Vietnam. They had the political power and popularity to have made it
happen, too. All three were also determined to advance integration and equal rights, and push for more spending on domestic
programs.

No one can guess what might have been achieved for the poor
and the dispossessed if Robert Kennedy had survived and been
elected president. Many people were firmly convinced he could
have bridged the divide between the races.

You can see it in their faces if you study the photographs of Kennedy's funeral train as it rolled slowly southward from New York's
Penn Station in to Union Station in Washington, D.C. Black, white,
Hispanic, young and old – they stood near the tracks, side by side,
tearful, united in their grief, some saluting, some waving American
flags. You can see it in their eyes: They knew that it wasn't just a
man who'd been killed, but a vision of a better America.

area close to their home, they freaked out. They opposed it like the plague.

At some point, millennials will have to make a similar choice. They will have to decide whether their impulse toward social justice and equal opportunity outweighs their desire to make the same "business decision" their elders made and protect their investment in a home by keeping out people who are poorer or of different races.

They will have to decide whether to give in to financial self-interest that manifests itself in exclusion or to act out of hope about the benefits of weaving a stronger fabric of community by inviting a mix of people to live and work together.

The path forward is not easy – whether at the national political level or in the city halls of local communities where land use decisions are made every day.

It helps to remember what Lyndon Johnson said about the spirit of America in his first inaugural address in 1965, just before HUD was created:

The essence of the American character is "the excitement of becoming – always becoming, trying, probing, falling, resting, and trying again – but always trying and always gaining."

HUD has been trying to advance American communities for 50 years with very good success. Now it's up to the rest of us to recognize what's at stake and to start helping.

It's tempting to undervalue the importance of what HUD does, but don't let its lackluster image fool you. And don't ignore the connection between its work and today's headlines about displaced tenants and police treatment of African Americans.

The more that affluent areas succeed in excluding lower-income folks and forcing them to remain in places of concentrated poverty, the more the gaps between groups will widen, with all the fear, distrust, and anger that brings.

Integration of housing by race and income cannot ensure peaceful social relationships, but housing segregation is guaranteed to make misunderstanding, mistrust, anger, and hostility much worse.

As usual, Martin Luther King, Jr., expressed it best. Speaking at Cornell College in Mt. Vernon, Iowa, in 1962, he said:

I am convinced that men hate each other because they fear each other. They fear each other because they don't know each other, and they don't know each other because they don't communicate

with each other, and they don't communicate with each other because they are separated from each other.

In the aftermath of violent demonstrations in Ferguson, Mo.,
and rioting in Baltimore in 2015, pundits and reporters have asked
the big question: Should we expect a resurgence of the kind of violence we saw in the 1960s?

It's impossible to predict if or when the lingering divisions between racial and income groups will lead to violent conflict.

What we know for certain is that the problems of concentrated
poverty and unaffordable housing have already damaged us economically and socially, just as we were warned they would 50 years ago.
We know that access to good housing and healthy communities is
essential to the American dream of upward mobility and to creating
better opportunities for each successive generation.

If people think that it's never going to happen for them, that
they will never move up and out of their overcrowded living space
and lousy neighborhood no matter how many hours they work at a
low-wage job, it destroys the idea of upward mobility. It makes the
promise of America – that anyone can succeed if they work hard
enough – less and less credible.

It sets up a situation that is eerily similar to how the residents of
the 1960s ghettos felt, that there is nowhere to go, no advancement,
that the doors to the "other America" are closed.

King did not dwell on the threat of violence, even though it was
often close at hand for him. He always spoke about what was possible
if everyone did all they could to advance social justice:

> Human progress never rolls in on the wheels of inevitability. It
> comes through the tireless efforts and the persistent work of dedi-
> cated individuals who are willing to be co-workers with God. And
> without this hard work, time itself becomes an ally of the primitive
> forces of social stagnation.

King said those words at the National Cathedral in Washington,
D.C., on March 29, 1968, six days before he was murdered and his
voice silenced.

Endnotes

SECTION I

Exodus & Upheaval

[1] Robert Weaver, *The Negro Ghetto* (New York: Harcourt, Brace, 1948), 29.

[2] National Advisory Commission on Civil Disorders, *Report of the National Advisory Commission on Civil Disorders* (New York: Bantam, 1968) [hereafter Kerner report].

[3] Kim-Mai Cutler, East of Palo Alto's Eden: Race and The Formation of Silicon Valley, techcrunch.com, posted Jan. 10, 2015

[4] Governor's Commission on the Los Angeles Riots. *Violence in the City: An End or a Beginning?* December 1965.

[5] Kerner report, 467.

[6] Ibid., 467.

[7] Ibid., 471.

[8] *Encyclopedia of Chicago*, s.v. "Blockbusting," by Arnold Hirsch, accessed May, 2015, http://www.encyclopedia.chicagohistory.org/pages/147.html.

[9] Kerner report, 467.

[10] Ibid., 246.

[11] Richard Rothstein, "Public Housing: Government-Sponsored Segregation," *American Prospect,* October 11, 2012, http://prospect.org/article/public-housing-government-sponsored-segregation.

[12] Ibid.

[13] Martha Biondi, *To Stand and Fight: The Struggle for Civil Rights in Postwar New York City* (Harvard University Press, 2006), 122.

[14] Laurence Glasco, "Double Burden: The Black Experience in Pittsburgh," in Samuel P. Hays, *City at the Point: Essays on the Social History of Pittsburgh* (Pittsburgh: University of Pittsburgh Press, 1989), 89.

[15] Kenneth Stahl, *The Great Rebellion: A Socio-economic Analysis of the 1967 Detroit Riot* (self published, 2009).

[16] Kerner report 142.

[17] Wendell E. Pritchett, *Robert Clifton Weaver and the American City: The Life and Times of an Urban Reformer* (Chicago: University of Chicago Press, 2008).

¹⁸ Ibid.

¹⁹ Ibid., 166, note 34.

²⁰ Clay Risen, *A Nation on Fire: America in the Wake of the King Assassination* (New York: Wiley, 2009).

²¹ Pritchett, *Robert Clifton Weaver,* 234–35.

²² Kerner report, 474.

²³ Thomas W. Hanchett, "The Other 'Subsidized Housing': Federal Aid to Suburbanization 1940s-1960s." in *From Tenements to the Taylor Homes: In Search of an Urban Housing Policy in Twentieth Century America.*

²⁴ CQ Almanac, 1967, 23rd ed., 13-503-13-505

²⁵ Charles Monroe Haar, *Between the Idea and the Reality: A Study in the Origin, Fate, and Legacy of the Model Cities Program* (New York: Little, Brown, 1975).

²⁶ *ubarchives* on Flickr, University of Baltimore, https://www.flickr.com/photos/ubarchives/sets/72157644227911580/; Accessed May 2015

²⁷ *BlackPast.org,* c.v. "The California Fair Housing Act/The Rumford Act (1963–1968)," by Herbert G. Ruffin, II, http://www.blackpast.org/aaw/california-fair-housing-act-rumford-act-1963-1968#sthash.6xzQflpQ.dpuf.

²⁸ Governor's Commission on the Los Angeles Riots. *Violence in the City: An End or a Beginning?* December 1965. http://www.usc.edu/libraries/archives/cityinstress/mccone/contents.html.

²⁹ Dennis L. Breo, "July 14, 1966," *Chicago Tribune,* July 6, 1986. http://articles.chicagotribune.com/1986-07-06/features/8602180464_1_bunk-bed-nurses-townhouse)

³⁰ Ellis Cose, "Why I Write," *Newsweek,* November 10, 2007, http://www.newsweek.com/why-i-write-96805.

³¹ Kerner report, 68.

³² Ibid.

³³ Ibid.

³⁴ Ibid.

³⁵ *Wikipedia,* s.v. "Robert F. Kennedy's Speech on the Assassination of Martin Luther King," last modified April 8, 2015, http://en.wikipedia.org/wiki/Robert_F._Kennedy%27s_speech_on_the_assassination_of_Martin_Luther_King,_Jr.

³⁶ Risen, *Nation on Fire.*

³⁷ Ibid.

[38] Robert F. Kennedy, "Remarks at the University of Kansas, March 18, 1968 (transcription of speech, John F. Kennedy Library), http://www.jfklibrary.org/Research/Research-Aids/Ready-Reference/RFK-Speeches/Remarks-of-Robert-F-Kennedy-at-the-University-of-Kansas-March-18-1968.aspx.

[39] Jack Newfield, *RFK: A Memoir* (New York: Nation Books, 2003).

[40] Risen, *Nation on Fire.*

[41] Michael Yokel, "100 Years: The Riots of 1968," *Baltimore Magazine* (May 2007), http://www.baltimoremagazine.net/features/2007/05/100-years-the-riots-of-1968.

[42] Kerner report, 398.

SECTION II

The Slippery Slope of Stalled Progress

[1] RealtyTrac staff, "1.1 Million U.S. Properties with Foreclosure Filings in 2014, Down 18 Percent from 2013 to Lowest Level since 2006," RealtyTrac website, January 14, 2015, http://www.realtytrac.com/news/foreclosure-trends/1-1-million-u-s-properties-with-foreclosure-filings-in-2014-down-18-percent-from-2013-to-lowest-level-since-2006/.

[2] Bipartisan Policy Center, "Housing America's Future: New Directions for National Policy" (Washington, DC: Bipartisan Policy Center, February 2013).

[3] Ibid.

[4] Debbie Gruenstein Bocian, "The State of Lending in America and Its Impact on U.S. Households" (Research report, Center for Responsible Lending, Durham, NC, December 2012).

[5] Jacob S. Rue, Len Albright, and Douglas S. Massey, "Race, Space, and Cumulative Disadvantage: A Case Study of the Subprime Lending Collapse," *Social Problems* 62, no. 2 (May 2015): 186–218.

[6] "National Homeownership Month, 2005" (proclamation by the President of the United States of America, May 25, 2005), http://georgewbush-whitehouse.archives.gov/news/releases/2005/05/20050525-14.html.

[7] Government Accountability Office, "Growing Number Increases Communities" Costs and Challenges" (Report GAO-12-34, submitted to the Committee on Oversight and Government Reform, House of Representatives, November 4, 2011).

[8] Ibid.

[9] Spencer Cowan and Michael Aumiller, "Unresolved Foreclosures: Patterns of Zombie Properties in Cook County" (Report, Woodstock Institute Chicago, IL, January 2014).

[10] Patrick Sharkey, *Stuck in Place: Urban Neighborhoods and the End of Progress Toward Racial Equality* (Chicago: University of Chicago Press, 2013).

[11] Joe Cortright, "Lost in Place: Why the Persistence and Spread of Concentrated Poverty—Not Gentrification—Is Our Biggest Urban Challenge," *CityObservatory,* September 12, 2014, http://cityobservatory.org/lost-in-place/.

[12] Cortright, "Lost in Place."

[13] Algernon Austin, "The Unfinished March" (report prepared for the Economic Policy Institute, Washington, DC, June 18, 2013).

[14] Ed Glaeser, "Ghettos: The Changing Consequences of Ethnic Isolation," *Regional Review* 7, no. 2 (Spring, 1997), http://www.bostonfed.org/economic/nerr/rr1997/spring/glsr97_2.htm.

[15] Douglas Massey and Nancy Denton, *American Apartheid: Segregation and the Making of the Underclass* (Cambridge, MA: Harvard University Press, 1998).

[16] Jacob S. Rue and Douglas S. Massey, "Segregation in Post–Civil Rights America: Stalled Integration or End of the Segregated Century?," *Du Bois Review* 11, no. 2 (2014): 205–32.

[17] "New Racial Segregation Measures for Large Metropolitan Areas: Analysis of the 1990–2010 Decennial Censuses" (Population Studies Center website, University of Michigan, 2015), http://www.psc.isr.umich.edu/dis/census/segregation2010.html.

[18] John R. Logan and Brian Stults, "The Persistence of Segregation in the Metropolis: New Findings from the 2010 Census" (National Center for Biotechnology Information, Bethesda MD, 2011).

[19] Glaeser, "Ghettos."

[20] Lois M. Quinn and John Pawasarat, "Racial Integration in Urban America: A Block Level Analysis of African American and White Housing Patterns" (research update, Employment and Training Institute, University of Wisconsin–Milwaukee, December 2002, revised January 2003), https://www4.uwm.

edu/eti/integration/integration.htm.

[21] Gary Orfield and Erica Frankenberg, with Jongyeon Ee and John Kuscera, "Brown at 60: Great Progress, a Long Retreat and an Uncertain Future" (Civil Rights Project, May 15, 2014).

[22] Carmen DeNavas-Walt and Bernadette D. Proctor, "Income and Poverty in the United States: 2013" (Current Population Report P60-249, Washington, DC: US Census Bureau, September 2014).

[23] US Commission on Civil Rights, "Equal Opportunity in Suburbia" (report presented to the US Congress, July 1974).

[24] Elizabeth Kneebone and Alan Berube, *Confronting Suburban Poverty in America* (Washington, DC: Brookings Institution Press, 2013).

[25] U.S. Census Bureau, American Community Survey.

[26] Joint Center for Housing Studies of Harvard University, *The State of the Nation's Housing 2014* (Cambridge, MA: Joint Center for Housing Studies, Harvard University, 2014).

[27] Rakesh Kochhar and Richard Fry, "Wealth Inequality Has Widened along Racial, Ethnic Lines since End of Great Recession" (report prepared for the Pew Research Center, Washington, DC, December 12, 2014), http://www.pewresearch.org/fact-tank/2014/12/12/racial-wealth-gaps-great-recession/.

[28] Joint Center for Housing Studies of Harvard University, *America's Rental Housing: Meeting Challenges, Building on Opportunities* (Cambridge, MA: Joint Center for Housing Studies, Harvard University, 2011).

[29] Advisory Commission on Regulatory Barriers to Affordable Housing, "'Not in My Backyard': Removing Barriers to Affordable Housing" (Washington, DC: Department of Housing and Urban Development, 1991).

[30] Downs, Anthony, "The Advisory Commission on Regulatory Barriers to Affordable Housing: Its Behavior and Accomplishments," *Housing Policy Debate* 2, no. 4 (1991): 1095—1137.

[31] US Commission on Equal Rights, "Equal Opportunity in Suburbia."

[32] Bipartisan Policy Center, "Housing America's Future."

SECTION III

The Politics of Fear

[1] Letter to the Speaker of the House Urging Enactment of the Fair

Housing Bill.
April 5, 1968, http://www.presidency.ucsb.edu/ws/index.
php?pid=28785

2 Housing and Urban Development Act of 1968

3 426 - Remarks Upon Signing the Housing and Urban Development Act of 1968.
August 1, 1968, http://www.presidency.ucsb.edu/ws/?pid=29056

4 Ibid.

5 Rick Pearlstein, *Nixonland: The Rise of a President and the Fracturing of America* (New York: Scribner, 2009).

6 Ibid.

7 Ibid.

8 Ibid.

9 Inaugural Address, January 20, 1969, http://www.presidency.ucsb.
edu/ws/index.php?pid=1941

10 Pritchett, *Robert Clifton Weaver*

11 Dean J. Kotlowski, *Nixon's Civil Rights: Politics, Principle, and
Policy* (Cambridge, MA: Harvard University Press, 2002).

12 Gregory D. Squires in *Segregation: The Rising Costs For America*,
Edited by James H. Carr and Nandinee K. Kutty, 2008

13 Rachel G. Bratt, "A Withering Commitment" (*Shelterforce
Online*, National Housing Institute, July/August 1997), http://
www.nhi.org/online/issues/94/bratt.html.

14 "Housing and Urban Development (HUD) Influence-
Peddling Scandal Unfolds before Hill Panels," *CQ Almanac*,
1989, http://library.cqpress.com/cqalmanac/document.
php?id=cqal89-1139712.

15 HUD web site

16 *Sustainable Communities* magazine

17 HUD web site

18 The Community Development Block Grant (CDBG) Program:
Fact Sheet (Nebraska Department of Economic Development),
http://www.neded.org/community/grants/applications/cdbg-
forms#2015GuideLines, accessed May 2015.

19 US Department of Housing and Urban Development, "The Community Development Block Grant (CDBG) Program's 40th
Anniversary" (*HUD.gov*), http://portal.hud.gov/hudportal/
HUD?src=/program_offices/comm_planning/communitydevel-
opment/CDBG_Turns_40, accessed May 2015.

20 Lawrence L. Thompson, "A History of HUD" (paper prepared for

the National Leased Housing Association, 2006), http://hudn-lha.com/wp-content/uploads/documents/hud_history.pdf.

[21] The 2013 Annual Homeless Assessment Report (AHAR) to Congress

[22] Northeastern Ohio Sustainable Communities Consortium press release

[23] Bipartisan Policy Center, "Housing America's Future"

[24] Federal Reserve Board, *Federal Reserve Bulletin* "Changes in U.S. Family Finances from 2010 to 2013," in

[25] Report of the Commission on Affordable Housing and Health Facility Needs for Seniors

[26] Joint Committee on Taxation staff, "Estimates of Federal Tax Expenditures for Fiscal Years 2014–2018" (Report prepared for the Joint Committee on Taxation, August 5, 2014), http://www.jct.gov/publications.html?func=startdown&id=4663.

[27] Ibid.

[28] Prepared Remarks for Secretary of Housing and Urban Development Shaun Donovan at the Brookings Institution Metropolitan Policy Program's Discussion - "From Despair to Hope: Two HUD Secretaries on Urban Revitalization and Opportunity, July 14th, 2009. http://www.hud.gov/news/speeches/2009-07-14.cfm

Bibliography

Advisory Commission on Regulatory Barriers to Affordable Housing. "'Not in My Backyard': Removing Barriers to Affordable Housing." Washington, DC: Department of Housing and Urban Development, 1991.

Apgar, William C., Jr., Mark Duda, and Rochelle Nawrocki Gorey. "The Municipal Cost of Foreclosures: A Chicago Case Study." Housing Finance Policy Research Paper No. 2005-01, Homeownership Preservation Foundation, Minneapolis, Minnesota, February 2005. http://www.nw.org/network/neighborworksProgs/foreclosuresolutionsOLD/documents/2005Apgar-DudaStudy-FullVersion.pdf.

Apgar, William C., Jr., Christopher E. Herbert, and Priti Mathur. "Risk or Race: An Assessment of Subprime Lending Patterns in Nine Metropolitan Areas." Research report, U.S. Department of Housing and Urban Development, Office of Policy Development and Research, Washington, D.C., August 2011. http://www.huduser.org/Publications/pdf/risk_race_2011.pdf.

Arik, Hulya, "The Social and Economic Impacts of Affordable Housing Development." Research report, Tennessee Housing Development Agency, Nashville, TN, May 2010.

Arnquist, Sarah. "The Million Dollar (Homeless) Patient: Calculating the Health Care Costs of Chronic Homelessness." Online report, *Reporting on Health,* USC Annenberg School of Journalism, USC, n.d. http://www.reportingonhealth.org/resources/lessons/million-dollar-homeless-patient.

Austin, Algernon. "The Unfinished March." Report prepared for the Economic Policy Institute, Washington, DC, June 18, 2013.

Bassuk, Ellen L., et al. "America's Youngest Outcasts 2010." National Center on Family Homelessness, Needham, MA, December 2011.

BcMiller, Haley, Courtney Jacquin, and Jakub Rudnik. "Finding Affordable Housing in Chicago Lawn: One Renter's Story." Institute for Housing Studies at DePaul University. Blog entry, December 20, 2013. http://www.housingstudies.org/news/blog/finding-affordable-housing-in-Chicago-Lawn/.

Bergen, Mark. "George Romney and the Last Gasps of Urban Policy." *Forbes,* February 28, 2012. http://www.forbes.com/sites/markbergen/2012/02/28/george-romney-and-the-last-gasps-of-national-urban-policy/.

Bibby, Douglas M. "A New and Sustainable Housing Policy." PowerPoint presentation. Washington, DC: National Multi Housing Council,

Bilbert, Ben and Washington Post Staff, *Ten Blocks from the White House: Anatomy of the Washington Riots of 1968* (Praeger, 1968).

Biondi, Martha Biondi. *To Stand and Fight: The Struggle for Civil Rights in Postwar New York City.* New York: Harvard University Press, 2006.

Bipartisan Millennial Housing Commission. "Meeting Our Nation's Housing Challenges." Report to Congress. Bipartisan Millennial Housing Commission, Washington, DC, May 2002.

Bipartisan Policy Center, Economic Policy Program, Housing Commission. "Housing America's Future: New Directions for National Policy." Washington, DC: Bipartisan Policy Center, February 2013.

BlackPast.org, c.v. "The California Fair Housing Act/The Rumford Act (1963–1968)." Herbert G. Ruffin, II, http://www.blackpast.org/aaw/california-fair-housing-act-rumford-act-1963-1968#sthash.6xzQflpQ.dpuf.

Bluestone, Barry, and Chase Billingham. "The Greater Boston Housing Report Card 2011: Housing's Role in the Ongoing Economic Crisis." Boston: The Boston Foundation, 2011.

Bocian, Debbie Gruenstein. "The State of Lending in America and Its Impact on U.S. Households." Research report, Center for Responsible Lending, Durham, NC, December 2012.

Bocian, Debbie Gruenstein, Wei Li, and Keith S. Ernst. "Foreclosures by Race and Ethnicity: The Demographics of a Crisis." Research report, Center for Responsible Lending, Durham, NC, June 18, 2010). www.responsiblelending.org/.../foreclosures-by-race-presentation.pdf.

Bocian, Debbie Gruenstein, Wei Li, Carolina Reid, and Roberto G. Quercia. "Lost Ground, 2011: Disparities in Mortgage Lending and Foreclosures." Research report, Center for Responsible Lending, Durham, NC, November 2011.
http://www.responsiblelending.org/mortgage-lending/research-analysis/lost-ground-2011.html.

Bocian, Debbie Gruenstein, Peter Smith and Wei Li. "Collateral Damage: The Spillover Costs of Foreclosures." Research report, Center for Responsible Lending, Durham, NC, October 24, 2012.
http://www.responsiblelending.org/mortgage-lending/research-analysis/collateral-damage.html.

Bravve, Elina, Megan Bolton, Linda Couch, and Sheila Crowley. *Out of Reach 2012: America's Forgotten Housing Crisis.* Washington, DC: National Low Income Housing Association, March 2012.

Breo Dennis L. "July 14, 1966." *Chicago Tribune,* July 6, 1986, http://articles.chicagotribune.com/1986-07-06/features/8602180464_1_bunk-bed-nurses-townhouse)

Brennan, Mary. "The Impacts of Affordable Housing on Education: A Research Summary." Research brief, Center for Housing Policy, May 2011.
www.nhc.org/media/files/Insights_HousingAndEducationBrief.pdf.

Business and Professional People for the Public Interest. "How Can Municipalities Confront the Vacant Property Challenge?" Business and Professional People for the Public Interest, Chicago Metropolitan Agency for Planning, and Metropolitan Mayors Conference, March 2010.
http://www.bpichicago.org/documents/HowCanMunicipalitiesConfrontthe-VacantPropertyChallenge_AnIntroductoryGuide-1.pdf.

California Reinvestment Coalition, Empire Justice Center, Massachusetts Affordable Housing Alliance, Neighborhood Economic Development Advocacy Project, Ohio Fair Lending Coalition, Reinvestment Partners, and Woodstock Institute. "Paying More for the American Dream VI: Racial Disparities in FHA/VA Financing." Research Report, July 2012.

www.nedap.org/resources/documents/payingmoreVI-7-19-12.pdf.

Campbell, John, Stefano Giglio, and Parag Pathak. "Forced Sales and House
Prices" *American Economic Review* 101, no. 5 (2011): 2108—31. https://
www.aeaweb.org/articles.php?doi=10.1257/aer.101.5.2108.

Carey, Nick. "Cheap Detroit Houses Scooped up by Investors Can Be Costly
for Communities, Bad News for Buyers, Reuters." *Huffington Post,*
July 3, 2013. http://www.huffingtonpost.com/2013/07/03/cheap-detroit-
houses_n_3538213.html.

Carr, James H., Katrin B. Anacker, and Ines Hernandez. "The State of Housing in Black America 2013." Lanham, MD: National Association of Real
Estate Brokers, 2013.

Carr, James H., and Nandinee K. Kutty, *Segregation: The Rising Costs For
America*, 2008

Carter, Jimmy. "Housing and Community Development Act of 1977 Remarks
on Signing H.R. 6655 Into Law," October 12, 1977. http://www.presidency.
ucsb.edu/ws/index.php?pid=6782&st=housing+and+community+develop
ment+act&st1=HUD.

Casey, Maura. "'A Fighting Chance,' by Elizabeth Warren." *Washington Post,*
April 21, 2014. http://www.washingtonpost.com/opinions/a-fighting-chance-
by-elizabeth-warren/2014/04/21/fb894b68-be9b-11e3-bcec-b71ee10e9bc3_
story.html.

Chakrabarti, Ritashree, and Junfu Zhang. "Unaffordable Housing and Local
Employment Growth." Working Paper 10-3, New England Public Policy
Center at the Federal Reserve Bank of Boston, Boston, 2010). http://www.
bos.frb.org/economic/neppc/wp/2010/neppcwp103.pdf.

Community Builders staff. "The Promise of Mixed-Income Communities."
Boston, MA: Community Builders, 2007.

Corkery, Michael. "Wall Street's New Housing Bonanza." Dealbook, January
29, 2014.
http://dealbook.nytimes.com/2014/01/29/wall-streets-new-housing-bonan-
za/?_php=true&_type=blogs&_r=0.

Cortes, Alvaro, Meghan Henry, RJ de la Cruz, Scott Brown, Jill Khadduri, and
Dennis P. Culhane. "The 2012 Point-in-Time Estimate of Homelessness:
Vol. I of the 2012 Annual Homelessness Assessment Report." The Selected
Works of Dennis P. Culhane, 2012. http://works.bepress.com/dennis_cul-
hane/120.

Cortright, Joe. "Lost in Place: Why the Persistence and Spread of Concentrated Poverty—Not Gentrification—Is Our Biggest Urban Challenge."
CityObservatory, September 12, 2014, http://cityobservatory.org/lost-in-
place/.

Cose, Ellis. "Why I Write," *Newsweek,* November 10, 2007.

Cowan, Spencer, and Michael Aumiller. "Unresolved Foreclosures: Patterns of Zombie Properties in Cook County." Report, Woodstock Institute Chicago, IL, January 2014.

Crosby, Jackie. "UnitedHealth Invests $50 Million in Low-Income Rental
Housing." *Star Tribune,* November 14, 2013. http://www.startribune.com/
business/231933561.html.

CQ Almanac. "Housing and Urban Development (HUD) Influence-Peddling
    Scandal Unfolds before Hill Panels." 1989,   http://library.cqpress.com/
    cqalmanac/document.php?id=cqal89-1139712.
Crouch, Elisa. "Normandy Chorale Heads to Carnegie Hall." *St. Louis Post-
    Dispatch,* March 7, 2014. http://www.stltoday.com/news/local/education/
    normandy-chorale-heads-to-carnegie-hall/article_431284c7-a63f-53bf-a1a0-
    08ecc33693e1.html.
Culhane, D., W. Parker, B. Poppe, K. Gross, and E. Sykes. "Accountability, Cost-
    Effectiveness, and Program Performance: Progress since 1998." University
    of Pennsylvania, School of Social Policy and Practice, January 2008. http://
    repository.upenn.edu/cgi/viewcontent.cgi?article=1116&context=spp_pa-
    pers.
Culhane, Dennis P., John Fantuzzo, Whitney LeBoeuf, and Chin-Chih Chen.
    "Alternative Approach: Assessing the Impact of HUD's Assisted Housing
    Programs on Educational Opportunity and Well-being." Research report,
    U.S. Department of Housing and Urban Development, Office of Policy De-
    velopment and Research, Washington, D.C., August 11, 2011. http://www.
    huduser.org/portal/publications/pubasst/culhane_alternative.html.
Culhane, Dennis P., and Stephen Metraux. "Rearranging the Deck Chairs
    or Reallocating the Lifeboats? Homelessness Assistance and Its Al-
    ternatives." *Journal of the American Planning Association,* 74, no. 1
    (2008): 111—21.
    http://www.tandfonline.com/doi/full/10.1080/01944360701821618.
Culhane, Dennis P., Jung Min Park, and Stephen Metraux. "The Patterns and
    Costs of Services Use among Homeless Families." *Journal of Community
    Psychology* 39, no. 7 (September 2011) 815–25. Full text: http://works.
    bepress.com/dennis_culhane/104.
Cuomo, Andrew. "Secretary Andrew Cuomo's Remarks at the Dedication Cer-
    emony for the Robert C. Weaver Federal Building," Washington, DC, July
    11, 2000, HUD Archives.
    http://archives.hud.gov/remarks/cuomo/speeches/weaverspch.cfm.
Dawsey, Darrell. "To CHP Officer Who Sparked Riots, It Was Just Another
    Arrest." *LA Times,* August 19, 1991. http://articles.latimes.com/1990-08-19/
    local/me-2790_1_chp-officer.
DeNavas-Walt, Carmen, and Bernadette D. Proctor, "Income and Poverty in
    the United States: 2013." Current Population Report P60-249, Washing-
    ton, DC: US Census Bureau, September 2014.
Desloge, Rick. "Save-A-Lot Will Anchor $6 Million Beyond Housing Develop-
    ment." *St. Louis Business Journal,* November 6, 2009. http://www.iff.org/
    %2Fresources%2Fcontent%2F4%2F6%2Fdocuments%2FSt%20Louis%20
    Business%20journal_11_6_091.pdf.
Downs, Anthony. "The Advisory Commission on Regulatory Barriers to Af-
    fordable Housing: Its Behavior and Accomplishments." *Housing Policy
    Debate* 2, no. 4 (1991): 1095–1137.
Dunford, James et al. "Impact of the San Diego Serial Inebriate Program on
    Use of Emergency Medical Resources." *Annals of Emergency Medicine* 47,
    no. 4 (April, 2006): 328-336.

http://www.sandiego.gov/sip/pdf/Impact%20of%20San%20Diego%20
SIP%20on%20Emergency%20Medical%20Resources.pdf.

Encyclopedia of Chicago, s.v. "Blockbusting," by Arnold Hirsch, http://
www.encyclopedia.chicagohistory.org/pages/147.html.

Fischer, Greg, Office of. "Mayor, Attorney General Announce National
Mortgage Foreclosure Settlement." News release by Mayor Greg Fischer,
Louisville, Kentucky, July 30, 2012. http://www.louisvilleky.gov/Mayor/
News/2012/7-30-12+mortgage+settlement.htm.

Fischer, Will. "Research Shows Housing Vouchers Reduce Hardship and
Provide Platform for Long-Term Gains among Children." Research report
prepared for the Center on Budget and Policy Priorities, Washington, DC,
March 10, 2014. http://www.cbpp.org/files/3-10-14hous.pdf.

Flaming, Daniel, Daniel Michael Matsunaga and Patrick Burns. "Where We
Sleep: The Costs of Housing and Homelessness in Los Angeles." Report
prepared for the Los Angeles Homeless Services Authority, November
2009. http://www.economicrt.org/summaries/Where_We_Sleep.html.

Gabriel, Stuart A. and Stuart S. Rosenthal. "The Boom, the Bust, and the Future of Home Ownership (revised)." Working paper 2013-13, Ziman Center
for Real Estate, UCLA, August 21, 2013. http://www.anderson.ucla.edu/
Documents/areas/ctr/ziman/2013-13WP.pdf.

Gallagher, Jim. "St. Louis Is Hot Spot for 'Underwater' Mortgages." *St. Louis
Post-Dispatch*, May 9, 2014. http://www.stltoday.com/business/local/st-louis-
is-hot-spot-for-underwater-mortgages/article_1a9b46b5-38f4-5b93-b4b4-
e895f8e0bab5.html.

Glaeser, Ed. "Ghettos: The Changing Consequences of Ethnic Isolation." *Regional Review* 7, no. 2 (Spring, 1997), http://www.bostonfed.org/economic/
nerr/rr1997/spring/glsr97_2.htm.

Glasco, Laurence (1989). "Double Burden: The Black Experience in Pittsburgh." In Samuel P. Hays, *City at the Point: Essays on the Social History of Pittsburgh*. Pittsburgh: University of Pittsburgh Press.

Government Accountability Office. "Growing Number Increases Communities" Costs and Challenges." Report GAO-12-34, submitted to the Committee on Oversight and Government Reform, House of Representatives,
November 4, 2011.

Government Accountability Office staff. "Vacant Properties: Growing Number
Increases Communities' Costs and Challenges." Report GAO-12-34. Washington, DC: Government Accountability Office, November 2011.

Governor's Commission on the Los Angeles Riots. *Violence in the City: An End
or a Beginning?* December 1965.

Habitat for Humanity. "Building toward 1 Million and So Much More: Habitat
for Humanity International Annual Report for FY2013." Habitat for Humanity, Atlanta, GA, 2013. http://www.habitat.org/sites/default/files/annual-
report-2013.pdf.

Han, Hye-Sung "The Impact of Abandoned Properties on Nearby Homes."
Housing Policy 24, no. 2 (2014): 311—34. http://www.tandfonline.com/doi/
abs/10.1080/10511482.2013.832350#.UzcmKvldXa4.

Haar, Charles Monroe. *Between the Idea and the Reality: A Study in the*

Origin, Fate, and Legacy of the Model Cities Program. New York: Little,
    Brown, 1975.

Hedberg William, and John Kraimer. "Credit Access Following a Mortgage
    Default," *Economic Research.* Federal Reserve Bank of San Francisco,
    October 29, 2012. http://www.frbsf.org/economic-research/publications/
    economic-letter/2012/october/credit-access-following-a-mortgage-default/.

Hickey, Robert, Jeffrey Lubell, Peter Haas, and Stephanie Morse. "Losing
    Ground: The Struggle of Moderate-Income Households to Afford the Rising
    Costs of Housing and Transportation." Research report prepared for the
    Center for Housing Policy, Washington, DC, and the Center for Neigh-
    borhood Technology, Chicago, October 2012. http://www.cnt.org/media/
    CNT_LosingGround.pdf.

Hoak, Amy "How Foreclosure Baacklogs Could Hurt Home Buyers: Slow Pro-
    cessing Could Keep Prices Down and Mortgage Rates Up." MarketWatch,
    December 3, 2012. http://www.marketwatch.com/story/how-foreclosure-
    backlogs-could-hurt-home-buyers-2012-12-03.

Home Defenders League (in Huffington Post). "Foreclosure Horror Story:
    Bank of America Mortgage Modification Allegedly Goes Wrong, March 12,
    2013. http://www.huffingtonpost.com/home-defenders-league/foreclosure-
    horror-story-bank-america_b_2862824.html.

Home Defenders League website. *100 Stories of What Wall Street Broke* web-
    site. http://100storiesofwhatwallstreetbroke.tumblr.com/.

Home Wreckers. "How Wall Street Foreclosures Are Devastating Ohio Com-
    munities." Ohio Organizing Collaborative and Service Employees Interna-
    tional Union, September 2011.

http://fightforafaireconomy.org/files/2011/09/Home-Wreckers-FINAL.pdf.

Home Wreckers. "How Wall Street Foreclosures Are Devastating Communi-
    ties, March 16, 2011.

http://www.calorganize.org/sites/default/files/Home-Wreckers-Report-
    March-16-2011.pdf.

Immergluck, Dan. *Foreclosed: High-risk Lending, Deregulation, and the
    Undermining of America's Mortgage Market.* Ithaca, NY: Cornell University
    Press, 2009.

Immergluck, Dan, and Geoff Smith. "The External Costs of Foreclosure:
    The Impact of Single-Family Mortgage Foreclosures on Property Values."
    Housing Policy Debate 17, no. 1 (2006). http://findaforeclosurecoun-
    selor.net/network/neighborworksProgs/foreclosuresolutions/pdf_docs/
    hpd_4closehsgprice.pdf.

Johnson, Lyndon. "Message to the Congress Transmitting First Annual
    Report of the Department of Housing and Urban Development," April 17,
    1967. http://www.presidency.ucsb.edu/ws/index.php?pid=28204&st=depart
    ment+of+housing&st1=HUD.

———. "Remarks at the Dedication of the Department of Housing and Urban
    Development Building," September 9, 1968, American Presidency Project.
    http://www.presidency.ucsb.edu/ws/?pid=29105.

———. "Remarks at the Swearing In of Robert C. Weaver and Robert C. Wood
    as Secretary and Under Secretary of Housing and Urban Development,"

January 18, 1966. http://www.presidency.ucsb.edu/ws/index.php?pid=27493
&st=department+of+housing&st1=HUD.

————. "Remarks at the Signing of Bill Establishing a Department of Housing
and Urban Development," September 9, 1965.
http://www.presidency.ucsb.edu/ws/index.php?pid=27245&st=department
+of+housing&st1=HUD.

————. "Remarks upon Signing the Housing and Urban Development Act of
1968." Speech presented on August 1, 1968. *American Presidency Project,*
http://www.presidency.ucsb.edu/ws/?pid=29056.

————. "Statement by the President upon Nominating the Incorporators
of the National Housing Partnership," September 9, 1968. http://www.
presidency.ucsb.edu/ws/index.php?pid=29106&st=department+of+housin
g&st1=HUD.

Joint Center for Housing Studies of Harvard University. *America's Rental
Housing: Meeting Challenges, Building on Opportunities.* Cambridge, MA:
Joint Center for Housing Studies, Harvard University, 2011.

————. "Key Facts," in *America's Rental Housing: Evolving Markets and
Needs.* Harvard University, December 9, 2013.
http://www.jchs.harvard.edu/sites/jchs.harvard.edu/files/americasrental-
housing-2013-factsheet_0.pdf.

————. *The State of America's Housing 2013.* Cambridge, MA: Joint Center
for Housing Studies, Harvard University, 2013.

————. "The State of the Nation's Housing: 2011." Research report, Joint
Center for Housing Studies, Cambridge, MA, June 14, 2012.
http://www.jchs.harvard.edu/research/publications/state-
nation%E2%80%99s-housing-2011.

Joint Economic Committee of Congress. "Foreclosure predictions." April 2008.
http://www.jec.senate.gov/public/?a=Files.Serve&File_id=0c77e023-746d-
4f57-bf8b-a595a7864371.

————. "The Full Subprime Mortgage Market Crisis Timeline 2006-2008."
July 2008.
http://www.jec.senate.gov/public/?a=Files.Serve&File_id=4cdd7384-dbf6-
40e6-adbc-789f69131903.

————. "Report Update: Sheltering Neighborhoods from the Subprime Foreclosure Storm." June 2007.
http://www.jec.senate.gov/public/?a=Files.Serve&File_id=389d9fc3-d503-
4168-9b11-2d73f3757ca8.

————. "Sheltering Neighborhoods from the Subprime Foreclosure Storm."
April 2007.
http://www.jec.senate.gov/public/?a=Files.Serve&File_id=8c3884e5-2641-
4228-af85-b61f8a677c28.

————. "The Subprime Lending Crisis: The Economic Impact on Wealth,
Property Values and Tax Revenues, and How We Got Here." Report and
Recommendations by the Majority Staff of the Joint Economic Committee,
Senator Charles E. Schumer, Chairman, Representative Carolyn B. Malo-
ney, Vicechair, October 2007. http://www.jec.senate.gov/archive/Documents/
Reports/10.25.07OctoberSubprimeReport.pdf.

———. "Subprime Mortgage Market Crisis Timeline." July 2008.
    http://www.jec.senate.gov/public/?a=Files.Serve&File_id=c20f56ef-5d57-
    4d1b-ba91-c5e5f373f9a9.
Kaiser, Edgar F., et al. *The Report of the President's Committee on Urban Hous-
    ing: A Decent Home.* Washington, DC: US Government Printing Office,
    1969.
Kennedy, Robert F. "Remarks at the University of Kansas, March 18, 1968.
    Ttranscription of speech, John F. Kennedy Library, http://www.jfklibrary.
    org/Research/Research-Aids/Ready-Reference/RFK-Speeches/Remarks-of-
    Robert-F-Kennedy-at-the-University-of-Kansas-March-18-1968.aspx.
Kingsley, G. Thomas, Robin Smith, and David Price. "The Impacts of Foreclo-
    sures on Families and Communities." Urban Institute, Washington, DC,
    May 2009.
Kirp, David. "Here Comes the Neighborhood." *New York Times*, October 19,
    2013. http://www.nytimes.com/2013/10/20/opinion/sunday/here-comes-the-
    neighborhood.html.
Kirp, David L., John P. Dwyer, and Larry A. Rosenthal. *Our Town: Race, Hous-
    ing, and the Soul of Suburbia.* New Brunswick, NJ: Rutgers University
    Press, 1997.
King, Martin Luther Jr. *Where Do We Go From Here: Chaos or Community?*
    Boston: Beacon, 1967.
Kneebone, Elizabeth, and Alan Berube. *Confronting Suburban Poverty in
    America.* Washington, DC: Brookings Institution Press, 2013.
———"Suburban Poverty Profiles: Montgomery County, Maryland."
    The Avenue/Rethinking Metropolitan America (blog), May 22, 2013.
    http://www.brookings.edu/blogs/the-avenue/posts/2013/05/22-suburban-
    poverty-kneebone-berube.
Kneebone, Elizabeth, Carey Nadeau, and Alan Berube. "The Re-Emergence
    of Concentrated Poverty: Metropolitan Trends in the 2000s." Metropoli-
    tan Opportunity Series, No. 25. Washington, DC: Brookings Institution,
    November 2011.
Kochhar, Rakesh, and Richard Fry. "Wealth Inequality Has Widened along
    Racial, Ethnic Lines since End of Great Recession." Pew Research Center,
    December 12, 2014.
Kotlowski, Dean J. *Nixon's Civil Rights: Politics, Principle, and Policy.* Cam-
    bridge, MA: Harvard University Press, 2002.
Landis, John D., and Kirk McClure. "Rethinking Federal Housing Policy."
    Journal of the American Planning Association 76, no. 3 (2010): 319–48.
Larimer, Mary E., et al. "Health Care and Public Service Use and Costs Before
    and After Provision of Housing for Chronically Homeless Persons with
    Severe Alcohol Problems." *Jama* 301 (2009): 1349—57.
Lauria, Mickey, and Erin Comstock. "The Effectiveness of Community Land
    Trusts." Working Paper no. WP07ML2, Lincoln Institute of Land Policy,
    Cambridge, MA, December 2007. http://www.lincolninst.edu/pubs/1313_
    The-Effectiveness-of-Community-Land-Trusts
Lewin Group. "Costs of Serving Homeless Individuals in Nine Cities." Chart
    book, prepared for the Partnership to End Long-Term Homelessness,

November 2004.

Lewit, Megan. "Homeless Cost Study." Research study for United Way of Greater Los Angeles, October 2009.
http://www.unitedwayla.org/wp-content/uploads/.../Homeless-Cost-Study.pdf

Logan, John R., and Brian Stults. "The Persistence of Segregation in the Metropolis: New Findings from the 2010 Census." National Center for Biotechnology Information, Bethesda, MD, 2011.

Martinez, T. E. and M. R. Burt. "Impact of Permanent Supportive Housing on the Use of Acute Care Health Services by Homeless Adults." *Psychiatric Services* 57, no. 7 (July 2006): 992—99.

Masnick, George S., Daniel McCue, and Eric S. Belsky. "Updated 2010 2020 Household and New Home Demand Projections." Joint Center for Housing Studies, Harvard University, Cambridge, MA, September 2010.

Massey, Douglas, and Nancy Denton. *American Apartheid: Segregation and the Making of the Underclass.* Cambridge, MA: Harvard University Press, 1998.

Massey, Douglas S. "Lessons from Suburbia." *Pathways* (Spring 2013): 19 23.

Massey, Douglas S., et al. *Climbing Mount Laurel: The Struggle for Affordable Housing and Social Mobility in an American Suburb.* Princeton: Princeton University Press, 2013.

Minnesota Community Land Trust Coalition website, http://www.mncltc.org/.

Mueller, Elizabeth J., and Alex Schwartz. "Reversing the Tide: Will State and Local Governments House the Poor as Federal Direct Subsidies Decline?" *Journal of the American Planning Association*, 74, no. 1 (2008): 122—35.
http://www.newschool.edu/uploadedFiles/Milano/.../schwartz_Mueller_Japa.pdf.

National Advisory Commission on Civil Disorders. *Report of the National Advisory Commission on Civil Disorders.* New York: Bantam, 1968.

National Alliance to End Homelessness. "The State of Homelessness in 2013: An Examination of Homelessness, Economic, Housing, and Demographic Trends at the National and State Levels." Research report, Homelessness Research Institute, April 8, 2013.
http://www.endhomelessncss.org/library/entry/the-state-of-homeless-ness-2013

National Community Land Trust Network, website, http://cltnetwork.org/.

National Center on Family Homelessness. "The Cost of Homelessness." Research brief prepared for Campaign to End Child Homelessness, National Center on Family Homelessness, December 2012.

National Housing Trust. "Housing Data." http://www.nhtinc.org/housing_data.php.

Newfield, Jack. *RFK: A Memoir.* New York: Nation Books, 2003.

"New Racial Segregation Measures for Large Metropolitan Areas: Analysis of the 1990–2010 Decennial Censuses." Population Studies Center website, University of Michigan, http://www.psc.isr.umich.edu/dis/census/segregation2010.html.

Orfield, Gary, and Erica Frankenberg, with Jongyeon Ee and John Kuscera.

"Brown at 60: Great Progress, a Long Retreat and an Uncertain Future."
Civil Rights Project, May 15, 2014.

Pearlstein, Rick. *Nixonland: The Rise of a President and the Fracturing of America*. New York: Scribner, 2009.

Pendall, Rolf, et al. "Demographic Challenges and Opportunities for U.S. Housing Markets." Washington, DC: Bipartisan Policy Center, 2013.

Phillips-Fein, Kim. "Living for the City: Robert Weaver's Liberalism." *Nation*, January 12, 2009. http://www.thenation.com/article/living-city-robert-clifton-weavers-liberalism?page=0,2.

Pietila, Antero. *Not in My Neighborhood: How Bigotry Shaped a Great American City*. Lanham, MD: Ivan R. Dee, 2010.

Pritchett, Wendell E. *Robert Clifton Weaver and the American City: The Life and Times of an Urban Reformer.* Chicago: University of Chicago Press, 2008.

Quinn, Lois M., and John Pawasarat. "Racial Integration in Urban America: A Block Level Analysis of African American and White Housing Patterns." Research update, Employment and Training Institute, University of Wisconsin–Milwaukee, December 2002, revised January 2003, https://www4.uwm.edu/eti/integration/integration.htm.

RealtyTrac staff, "1.1 Million U.S. Properties with Foreclosure Filings in 2014, Down 18 Percent from 2013 to Lowest Level since 2006." RealtyTrac website, January 14, 2015, http://www.realtytrac.com/news/foreclosure-trends/1-1-million-u-s-properties-with-foreclosure-filings-in-2014-down-18-percent-from-2013-to-lowest-level-since-2006/.

Reitman, Valerie and Mitchell Landsberg, "Watts Riots, 40 Years Later." *Los Angeles Times*, August 11, 2005. http://articles.latimes.com/2005/aug/11/local/la-me-watts11aug11.

Risen, Clay. *A Nation on Fire: America in the Wake of the King Assassination*. New York: Wiley, 2009.

Rugh, Jacob S., and Douglas S. Massey, "Segregation in Post–Civil Rights America: Stalled Integration or End of the Segregated Century?," *Du Bois Review* 11, no. 2 (2014): 205–32.

Rugh, Jacob S., Len Albright, and Douglas S. Massey. "Race, Space, and Cumulative Disadvantage: A Case Study of the Subprime Lending Collapse." *Social Problems*, 62, no. 2 (May 2015): 186–218.

Rothstein, Richard. "Public Housing: Government-Sponsored Segregation." *American Prospect,* October 11, 2012, http://prospect.org/article/public-housing-government-sponsored-segregation.

Satter, Beryl. *Family Properties: How the Struggle Over Race and Real Estate Transformed Chicago and Urban America*. New York: Picador, 2010.

Sauter, Michael B. "Cities with the Most Homes in Foreclosure." *24/7 Wall St.,* May 22, 2012.
http://247wallst.com/special-report/2012/05/22/large-cities-ruined-by-foreclosures/.

Scally, Corriene Payton, and Richard Koenig. "Beyong NIMBY and Poverty Deconcentration: Reframing the Outcomes of Affordable Rental Housing Development." *Ideas* 22, no. 3 (February 2012): 435—61. http://hdl.handle.

net/10.1080/10511482.2012.680477

Schildkraut, Jaclyn, and Elizabeth Erhardt Mustaine. "Movin', but Not up to the East Side: Foreclosures and Social Disorganization in Orange County, Florida." Housing Studies 29, no. 2 (2013): 177—97. http://www.tandfonline.com/doi/full/10.1080/02673037.2014.848263#.Uy3xjvldXa4.

Schmit, Julie. "Report Estimates 8 Million Children Hurt by Foreclosures." USA Today, April 18 2012. http://usatoday30.usatoday.com/money/economy/housing/story/2012-04-18/foreclosure-impact-on-children/54396706/1.

Schor, Elana. "Washington's Black Community Remembers the 1968 Riots." Guardian, 4 April, 2008. http://www.theguardian.com/world/2008/apr/04/1968theyearofrevolt.usa.

Schuetz, Jenny, Rachel Meltzer, and Vicki Been. "Silver Bullet or Trojan Horse? The Effects of Inclusionary Zoning on Local Housing Markets in the United States." Urban Studies 48, no. 2 (February 2011): 297-329. Full text: www.hks.harvard.edu/var/ezp_site/storage/.../file/.../silver_bullet.pdf .

Schwartz, Heather. "Can Housing Policy Be Good Education Policy?" Pathways (Spring 2013): 24–27.

Sharkey, Patrick. Stuck in Place: Urban Neighborhoods and the End of Progress toward Racial Equality. Chicago: University of Chicago Press, 2013.

Shashaty, Andre F. "Help Us Shape Future of Federal Housing Policy." Affordable Housing Finance (March 2008): 24–26. http://www.housingfinance.com/affordable-housing/help-us-shape-future-of-federal-housing-policy.aspx.

———. "Contracting Out of Control? Questions Persist about HUD Contracting as Congress Investigates Political Influence." Affordable Housing Finance (March 2008): 36–50.

Shin, Annys. "In Prince George's, Hundreds of Vacant Houses Drag Down Neighborhoods." Washington Post, January 13, 2013. http://www.washingtonpost.com/local/in-prince-georges-hundreds-of-vacant-houses-plague-neighborhoods/2013/01/13/93c0c5ca-503c-11e2-950a-7863a013264b_story.html.

Shine, Conor. "Las Vegas Working on Way to Curb Blight of Foreclosure." Las Vegas Sun, November 16, 2011. http://www.lasvegassun.com/news/2011/nov/16/las-vegas-working-way-curb-blight-foreclosure/.

Smith, Geoff, and Sarah Duda. "The State of Rental Housing in Cook County." Institute for Housing Studies, DePaul University, Chicago, 2013.

Stahl, Kenneth. The Great Rebellion: A Socio-economic Analysis of the 1967 Detroit Riot. Self published, 2009.

Standley, Fred L., and Louis H. Pratt. Conversations with James Baldwin. Jackson, MS: University Press of Mississippi, 1989.

Sungu-Eryilmaz, Yesim, and Rosalind Greenstein, "A National Study of Community Land Trusts." Wworking paper no. WP07YS1, Lincoln Institute of Land Policy, 2007. http://cltnetwork.org/wp-content/uploads/2014/01/2007-A-National-Study-of-CLTs.pdf.

Sussingham, Robin. "Foreclosure Process Hammers Florida's Housing Market." NPR, February 4, 2013. http://www.npr.org/2013/02/04/170752042/

foreclosure-process-hammers-floridas-housing-market.

Turbov, Mindy, and Valerie Piper. "HOPE VI and Mixed-Finance Redevelop-
    ments: A Catalyst for Neighborhood Renewal—Atlanta Case Study." Wash-
    ington, DC: Brookings Institution Metropolitan Policy Program, 2005.

Urban Institute. "Expanding Housing Opportunities through Inclusionary
    Zoning: Lessons from Two Counties." Report prepared for the US Depart-
    ment of Housing and Urban Development, Office of Policy Development
    and Research, Washington, DC, December 2012. http://www.huduser.org/
    Publications/pdf/HUD-496_new.pdf.

Urban Land Institute (ULI). "White Flint/Rockville Pike, Montgomery
    County, Maryland." In *Shifting Suburbs: Reinventing Infrastructure for
    Compact Development*. Report prepared for the ULI, Washington, DC,
    2012, 28 31. http://uli.org/wp-content/uploads/ULI-Documents/Shifting-
    Suburbs.pdf.

US Census Bureau. American Community Survey.

———. *American Housing Survey for the United States: 2009*. Current Hous-
    ing Reports, Series H150/09. Washington, DC: US Government Printing
    Office, 2011.

US Commission on Civil Rights. "Equal Opportunity in Suburbia." Report
    presented to the US Congress, July 1974.

US Conference of Mayors. "Hunger and Homelessness Survey: A Status
    Report on Hunger and Homelessness in America's Cities." Twenty-five-city
    survey, Washington, DC, December 2013.

www.usmayors.org/pressreleases/uploads/2013/1210-report-HH.pdf.

US Department of Housing and Urban Development, Office of Policy Develop-
    ment and Research. "Affordable Housing Needs 2005: Report to Congress."
    Washington, DC: Department of Housing and Urban Development, 2007.

———. "Worst Case Housing Needs 2011: Report to Congress." Washington,
    DC: Department of Housing and Urban Development, 2011.

Warren, Elizabeth. "Elizabeth Warren's 'A Fighting Chance': An Exclusive
    Excerpt on the Foreclosure Crisis." *Boston Globe*, April 27, 2014. http://
    www.bostonglobe.com/magazine/2014/04/26/elizabeth-warren-new-memoir-
    exclusive-excerpt-foreclosure-crisis/c02alOTRWXiYCMLxbakSiO/story.
    html?s_campaign=sm_tw.

Weaver, Robert. *The Negro Ghetto*. New York: Harcourt, Brace, 1948.

Westlund, Richard. "Workforce Housing in the New Economy." *BusinessMi-
    ami*, Fall 2012. bus.miami.edu/magazine/fall2012/features/workforce_hous-
    ing.html.

Williams, Roger, Mark Weinheimer, and James Brooks. "Resilience in the Face
    of Foreclosures: Six Case Studies on Neighborhood Stabilization." National
    League of Cities, Center for Research and Innovation, 2011.

Yokel, Michael. "100 Years: The Riots of 1968." *Baltimore Magazine*, May
    2007.

About This Book

This book lays out a story that spans a half-century since the mid-'60s riots and the creation of the Department of Housing and Urban Development to the present. The roots of the narrative go back close to 100 years, to the start of the Great Migration as African Americans started leaving the south to seek jobs with northern manufacturers during and right after World War I.

It is a story that's central to race relations in America. I hope the book encourages all who read it to devote more thought to the subject, and to see the deeper context of all the incidents of racial conflict in our society, including the heavily publicized cases involving law enforcement agencies' treatment of black men.

I know that deeply held beliefs about race change only slowly. This book asks only that you put aside your preconceptions long enough to look at the history as I've reported it and think about what it means.

The book is organized in three parts. Part One recounts the growth of the movement demanding fair housing and efforts to improve slum conditions in our cities, as well as the intense anger that erupted in riots starting most visibly in 1965. Part Two discusses current conditions, pointing out that segregation by race and income is still a problem today. Finally, Part Three talks about the achievements of federal housing and urban programs and the challenges they face, including strong political opposition.

This book is intentionally limited in scope. It is primarily about federal housing and urban policy. It is also concerned with civil rights, but primarily in the context of how housing is made available to some people and denied to others in America.

It recounts only a fraction of the violent conflict that occurred between Americans in the 1960s. It focuses on the major disturbances in northern cities that were part of the struggle for improvement in living conditions in the black ghettos, including equal housing opportunity, reform of federal urban programs, and affordable housing needs. It portrays these events in some detail in order to give younger readers a clear picture of the intensity of the violence of the period. However, it is not meant to be a full and objective history of the riots. Nor did I intend to endorse or condemn the violence. I relied heavily on official government documents and press accounts for the descriptions I used.

I left out any discussion of many other incidents of violence that were part of the struggle for civil rights. Other books have adequately documented the discrimination and violence perpetrated against African Americans during the civil rights struggle in the south.

Finally, this book's focus on housing and urban policy is not meant to suggest that it is not important to work on job creation, improvements to our educational system, or changes in law enforcement practices as they affect minorities. Those are all important.

In explanation, I wanted to keep this book focused on the story of how American urban and housing policy has evolved and where it stands today. I chose that focus because it is a policy area that gets very little attention in the popular media and on the bookshelves. In my view, it is the policy area with the most potential for government to have a significant impact in a relatively short time with a reasonable investment.

I regret that I could not describe the life of regular people who live in areas of concentrated poverty in detail. They are the missing Americans in our media-saturated culture. You don't hear about their struggles. They have no political power. Firsthand accounts of their struggles would be a great addition to this book, but there was no budget for visiting such places and talking to people.

For students of federal housing policy, including practitioners who struggle to work with HUD programs, I know that HUD gets in the way of local innovation almost as often as it encourages it. I know that there are massive problems at the agency.

One veteran of the Washington housing policy debate put it this way: "The main emphasis should shift from a bloated centralized Washington bureaucracy to rewarding and encouraging innovation and success at the state and local level — where the real action is."

I agree. However, after many years investigating and criticizing HUD as a journalist and publisher, I now recognize that eliminating HUD is not the way to get to that seemingly simple goal.

HUD's problems are serious but they can be addressed with strong leadership from the White House and a combination of financial resources and intelligent oversight from Congress (if future Congresses are capable of that, which I admit is a big unknown.) I hasten to add that I'm advocating less red tape and legal hurdles, not more.

HUD is the focal point for making progress on our housing and urban problems. Our challenge is to make it work better, not eliminate it. And today, with profound political choices coming up very soon, it holds the key to whether we continue or end our 50-year old commitment to creating communities of opportunity for people of all races and income levels.

Andre F. Shashaty

About the Author

I first started writing about federal housing and urban policy in the winter of 1979, when Jimmy Carter was president. A young journalist fresh from Ohio, I showed up at the Department of Housing and Urban Development eager to see how the best and brightest in government were solving our country's problems.

I was young and starry eyed. However, I was not alone in my belief in the capability of government. In my first years in the capital, I met many smart, energetic people who were working to continue the legacy of ambitious social programs left by President Lyndon Johnson. They still believed they could make a difference.

Coming from an all-white suburb in northeastern Ohio, I loved the urban lifestyle of Washington, D.C. But even as I expanded my social horizons and connected with a much more diverse group of friends, I also began to understand the reality of race relations as they played out in the geography of the region.

I remember walking along 14th Street in the northwestern section of the city. I was perplexed by the desolation I found there in 1979 – boarded up buildings, empty lots, and a lack of economic activity. Then I realized I had been walking in the place where the 1968 riots had taken place. The buildings had been burned and/or abandoned 11 years earlier.

The picture filled in further when I talked to white office workers who explained to me why they left their jobs on Capitol Hill and downtown the minute work hours ended and drove back to suburbia. They never stayed in the city after dark, and they did not come in on weekends. It was hard for me to believe, but they were still fearful of the city, long after the riots.

The dynamics of the process of how our cities are shaped and how we manage our housing markets and urban growth have fascinated me ever since. I have written regularly about HUD and housing and urban policy for most of the 36 years since my arrival in Washington.

My articles have been published in *The New York Times, The Washington Post*, and many other national papers and periodicals.

I am the author of the book, *Rebuilding a Dream: America's new urban crisis, the housing cost explosion, and how we can reinvent the American dream for all*. I have served as editor-in-chief of several magazines and journals, most recently including *Sustainable Communities* magazine.

I was founder, owner, and editor of *Affordable Housing Finance* magazine, the leading journal on government housing programs, as well as other real estate magazines and related conferences.

I have won awards and national media recognition for reporting on housing policy and the Department of Housing and Urban Development (HUD). My series of articles about corruption and favoritism in contracting at HUD in 2007 won a Neal Award from American Business Media, among other awards.

In Washington, D.C., I spent six years covering Congress and the federal agencies involved in housing for several periodicals, including serving as deputy editor of *Housing & Development Reporter*.

I spent six years in New York City, serving as editor-in-chief of a publication on commercial real estate and senior editor of a national magazine for the housing industry.

I am currently president of the Partnership for Sustainable Communities, a nonprofit based in San Rafael, Calif., that promotes urban planning and housing development strategies to advance social, economic, and environmental sustainability.

Andre F. Shashaty

About the Partnership for Sustainable Communities

The Partnership for Sustainable Communities (PSC) is a national 501(c)(3) nonprofit group that works at helping make American communities more economically, socially, and environmentally sustainable.

PSC educates policymakers and opinion leaders about the critical role of affordable housing located near jobs and transportation to the sustainability of American communities. PSC also advocates for revitalization of existing neighborhoods, preservation of existing housing, and improved energy efficiency.

PSC provides information, news, research, and advocacy tools via its website (www.p4sc.org). PSC also produces a regular electronic newsletter for members.

If you care about housing affordability and urban revitalization, support PSC. It's only $45 to become a member for one year. For information, go to www.p4sc.org or call 415-453-2100 x 302. Donations are tax-deductible to the full extent allowed by law.

The Partnership for Sustainable Communities was founded in 2009, and is not affiliated with the federal government's interagency partnership of the same name. PSC is a private nonprofit that receives no government support.

Another important book by Andre F. Shashaty

Rebuilding a Dream: *America's new urban crisis, the housing cost explosion, and how we can reinvent the American dream for all.*

"Rebuilding a Dream" puts the nation's housing and urban problems in perspective, explaining that we face a rapidly growing gap between what housing costs and what most Americans can afford to pay for shelter.

This new book from veteran journalist Andre Shashaty calls for a renewed commitment to housing and urban revitalization, and outlines steps that ordinary citizens can take to help bring that about.

"Rebuilding a Dream" has been selected as the 2015 book of the year by the National Association of Housing and Redevelopment Officials. It has received positive reviews from *Kirkus*, *Shelterforce* and many experts on housing policy.

Buy it now in PDF form at www.p4sc.org or in soft cover format at the Sustainability Bookstore *http://www.sustainabilitystore.org/*

The book is also available at Amazon for viewing on Kindle or the Cloud version of Kindle.

Bookstore and Library Buyers:

Rebuilding a Dream is available from Ingram.
ISBN: 978-0-9905187-0-9
Price: $29.95 before 50% discount
Publication Date: September, 2014
Publisher: Partnership for Sustainable Communities
Pages: 320

CPSIA information can be obtained
at www.ICGtesting.com
Printed in the USA
LVOW01s1714100716

495777LV00020B/395/P